Diary of a Witchcraft Shop

Trevor Jones and Liz Williams

Diary of a Witchcraft Shop

Trevor Jones and Liz Williams

Illustrated by Arthur Billington

NewCon Press
England

First published in the UK September 2011 by NewCon Press
41 Wheatsheaf Road, Alconbury Weston, Cambs, PE28 4LF

This edition, September 2012

www.newconpress.co.uk

NCP 042 (signed hardback)

NCP 043 (softback)

2nd edition

10 9 8 7 6 5 4 3 2

ISBN: 978-1-907069-85-7 (softback)

Cover art and internal illustrations by Arthur Billington

Cover layout and design by Andy Bigwood

Minor editorial meddling by Ian Whates

Book layout by Storm Constantine

Introduction

When you find yourself on a London platform shouting into your mobile, 'We haven't got enough demons! Do you want me to order some more?' as folk quietly edge away from you – you know you're running a witchcraft shop.

When one of your staff members believes herself to be Queen of the Fairies and tells all your suppliers of her new status as supernatural royalty – you know you're running a witchcraft shop.

When your customers think wormwood is for culinary purposes – you know you're running a witchcraft shop.

The Isle of Avalon, lost behind its mists, where Arthur was carried by three magical queens. Inis Witrin, the island of glass, ancient home of Christianity. Glastonbury, a little market town in Somerset. Whatever you call it, it's been a centre of pilgrimage and miracles for most of its history. People have been coming here for over a thousand years, looking for – *something*. Looking for Christ. Looking for the goddess or the god. Looking for angels and fairies. Looking for solutions and answers.

In 2004, when I was 39, I had a particularly bad Christmas. Over the course of ten days, my aunt died, a cousin was operated on for breast cancer, my father had a stroke, my then-boyfriend dumped me and so did my American publisher. Furthermore, it was the second anniversary of the death of my long-term partner, also from cancer: he'd died of a brain tumour on Christmas Eve, 2002.

So I did what a lot of people do. I came to Glastonbury, to get away from it all, to find some sort of healing. I went into the Goddess Temple, and there behind the altar was a representation of the Crone: the old bone woman of the heart of winter. It was too much, I told her: too much for me to cope with. And I gave my problems to her, like someone handing over a heavy piece of luggage.

Coming out of the Goddess Temple, I wandered around Glastonbury in the thin winter sunlight and found a little shop down an alley – like Diagon Alley in the Harry Potter novels. It was a little witchcraft shop, and standing in it was a big man who was kind enough to listen to all my woes. He gave me a meditation to do over Christmas, centred around blackthorn – the white-flowering, sloe-bearing purgative of the hedgerow. I did the meditation over Christmas, at my family's house. In the New Year, suffering from a dreadful cold, I came back to Glastonbury and went to see the big man in the little shop (it hadn't mysteriously vanished, by the way). He asked me out for a drink. We went to the George and Pilgrim hotel and talked about his bees, and that was that. Six years later, we're still together (along with two dogs, three cats, a Shetland and the aforementioned bees). The little shop became too little and we moved to Benedict Street: it's still there and it's called Witchcraft Ltd. Two more shops followed it, the Magick Box and the Cat and Cauldron (known to the occult cognoscenti as the Mog and Bucket: *thank* you for that, Jacquelyn in Lincoln).

Meeting Trevor wasn't the end of my problems. Fairy tales always have a dark aftermath. Over the next few years, we had more difficulties than many people experience in a lifetime. That was our Glastonbury Experience, of which later. But somehow, we're still sailing our little lifeboat through them all.

When I was with my late partner, Charles, we used to come to Glastonbury every year: he had old friends who ran the Assembly

Rooms. Charles hated shopping and wasn't all that keen on witchcraft, either (he was a Cabbalist: they don't seem to shop much). 'Welcome to bloody fairyland,' he'd say, as we pulled into St John's car park. So he would wait in the George and Pilgrim inn (700 years old and counting) while I rushed round the shops. There weren't so many witchcraft shops then, but I still never had enough time to look at things properly and I always wished I could spend more time in a shop in Glastonbury.

Be careful what you wish for, the old wives always say.

Sometimes, those old wives know what they're talking about.

October

Samhain

Evening comes quickly these days. I've been in Witchcraft Ltd all day, serving customers. There are lots of people around at the moment – it's Samhain, one of the major festivals of the pagan calendar. Working in the shop isn't just about selling things, though in many ways it's a standard retail operation. People also want to know about local moots, local covens, and at this time of year, which events are happening where. I've been directing folk up to the Chalice Well, which has a Samhain ceremony this evening, and also to the White Spring, that dark water-flowing cavern beneath the slopes of the Tor, turned into a wonderful shrine by the local community. They run moon ceremonies and of course, there's also the Goddess Temple who will be doing their own Samhain rite a day or so later.

The Temple is, at the time of writing, the UK's only place of worship that is dedicated to the goddess, in all her many forms. It's based around the idea of the Nine Morgens of Avalon – deities mentioned in the work of Isidore of Seville (though he suggests that Avalon was not, in fact, Glastonbury. But more of this later). You go up a flight of wooden steps in the courtyard of the Glastonbury Experience, take off your shoes, and pass inside into Goddess-space.

I went into the Temple this afternoon and found a quiet space behind webs of shadow, the bone-faced goddess smiling above the altar. It's a dark place right now, despite the numerous candles that throng the altar, signifying prayers for the ancestors at this season of the dead, and yet it's filled with a marvellous peace.

In quiet periods, I've been researching the season for our online radio show, the Witching Hour. The history of Samhain is murky, like all festivals. Conventional wisdom has it that Christianity stole many of the old pagan holidays. Sometimes that's true, sometimes – not so much. With Samhain, it's particularly difficult. There's very little evidence that the ancient Celts regarded it as the start of the New Year, as modern pagans do now. It seems to have been a festival based on the slaughter of cattle for the winter season. Sometimes tribes lit hilltop fires, sometimes not: it varied across Britain and Ireland.

A year before I wrote this, Trevor was finishing his treatment. Diagnosed on Lammas, with cancer of the throat, the course of radio- and chemotherapy was due to end on Samhain itself. Sometimes the gods give you very clear messages – a neon marker to an underworld trip.

The trouble is that by the time the actual festival comes around, we're all festivaled out. We're so busy enabling other people's Samhain that we forget to celebrate it ourselves – well, not quite. As I mentioned in the introduction to this book, I was widowed a few years ago, and since then Trevor and I estimate that we've lost about eleven people between us. A close friend of mine in his early 50s choked to death in the spring of 2004. Another died in the winter of 2003, of liver failure. Trevor has lost both parents in the last three years. The list goes on… So there are a lot of folk to remember.

We spend the early part of the evening in the George and Pilgrim hotel (known as the 'front office'), watching the revellers. By mutual consent we decide not to attend the ceremony at the Temple, purely because so many people have come into town for the occasion that we'd rather not take up the space that someone else could use. (This was written before the Goddess Temple acquired a new hall of their own.) But there are plenty of people in the pub, dressed in even more of a Gothic manner than usual.

I haven't dressed any differently to how I usually do, but I'm not sure that anyone can tell!

Later, we walk up the hill to the Chalice Well. It's freezing but you'd never think so, from the way the teenage girls at the bus stop are clad: all long bare legs and high heels. I don't know why they don't freeze. I sound like someone's mother. There are pumpkins all along the windowsills: Hallowe'en rather than Samhain. We've gone for a traditional window ourselves this year – though if we were really harking back to the folklore, it would have featured turnips. Shades of Baldrick. Perhaps best not to go there.

The well is beautiful in the darkness. We walk up through the shadows, flickering from hundreds of night lights, past the bare stems of chrysanthemums to the wellhead. We light a candle there: for death, for resurrection, for healing. And we remember the dead, in silence. Last night saw our own ceremony at home, in which a gate was opened in the veil between the worlds and the dead were asked to come through. The list of names is much too long. In our Druid grove this year – the private ritual rather than the public one at Stanton Drew stone circle – I took the part of the hag, the Cailleach, stepping hooded out of the night, calling the dead through the veil. But there's always light in the darkness. There's a bonfire blazing down on the lawn of the well gardens, not far from the twin yew trees and the hawthorn that seems so miraculously to bear fruit and flowers at the same time, like a tree in an old fairy tale. We walk down towards it, drawn by its fire, and then the story begins, the woman's voice, the voice of a professional storyteller, resonating through the gardens:

Once there was a young god, and his name was Balder the Beautiful…

The stories that are told are all different, and yet somehow always the same. We listen among the gathered crowd, breath frosting the air, under the damp darkness of the yews: Ioho, in the Celtic ogham alphabet, symbol of death and re-birth. Down at Nevern, in Pembrokeshire, the yew trees weep a bloody resin, so thick that their trunks look like flayed flesh. A grisly image, perhaps, but the Celts didn't flinch from death, and still don't. My father, also from Pembrokeshire, always told me that you could travel on the train from London to Haverfordwest and no one would speak, buried in their newspapers, until the train passed Gloucester and headed down the estuary into Wales. Then, around Cardiff, the conversation would start to pick up and by Carmarthen it would become more Welsh than English, and everyone would be talking about who had died. The story ends. Balder, struck through the heart by mistletoe, falls, and his death signals Ragnarok and the longest winter of all: Fimbulwinter, the apocalypse. But not yet.

We warm our hands at the fire for a moment, then walk back down through the town towards the lights and the car, our footsteps ringing on the hard cold ground.

We have just got back home after doing the shop window for Samhain. It is very witchy. I also had the following conversation:

Passing man, staring longingly at shop dummy: 'I've fancied her for, like, a really long time.'

Me: 'I have to tell you that her arms come off.'

Passing man: (after long thought) makes noise indicative of not really caring about dummy's detachable arms.

In 2006, Glastonbury was host to an event called *Youth 2000*. It's a Catholic youth movement, who parade through the town and then go up to the Tor, to 'purify' it. Whether or not the Tor needs purifying is a moot point, and the pagan community were up in arms about it. I'm of the opinion that it's the Christians' town too, and that the Catholics have suffered here as greatly as the pagan community – if not more so. Not that this justifies the 'purification,' however.

The march brought trouble, which hit the newspapers. Some lunatic went into one of the shops and threatened to set fire to the proprietress, who not unnaturally summoned the police. The nut in question turned out to have nothing to do with the march, and was subsequently cautioned for being illegally parked. Then he was thrown out of his guest house, so *Glastonbury = 1, fanatic = 0*, as far as we're concerned.

Trevor went to stand in front of the shop, to show solidarity, and the rest of the march passed peacefully enough, although everyone was plagued by shoplifting. On the day after it, I wrote to the local Catholic priest and asked if he'd like to come and visit us. When the priest showed up he turned out to be a delightful man who has a Wiccan aunty, so he's not under the impression that we're all Dennis Wheatley-style devil worshippers. We agreed to try and arrange an ecumenical picnic (this still hasn't happened, due to lack of time, but it's on the agenda).

Needless to say, the whole event got blown up out all proportion in the media. I had a call from a completely witless researcher from one of the national papers, and had to explain Catholicism, let alone the pagan side of things. Several years later, folk are still talking about it, which is a shame, because I don't hear them talking about how all the pagan businesses in town were asked by St John's church to contribute a Christmas tree to the church's annual tree festival (not an un-pagan event in itself, after all, when one considers the nature of Christmas trees), or how we've been officially invited to the induction of the new vicar.

Teenage Vampires

I was told the following story, which I hope is not apocryphal, last night by a regular at the Whitby Goth festival. A Yorkshire landlady has a teenage 'vampire' to stay during the festival. She issues him with a key to the door. That night, she's awoken by a call from the front garden. She looks out to see the teenage vampire.

'You've got a key, love!' she shouts down and closes the window.

Minutes later, there's a little stone thrown at the window. She looks out and there's the teenage vampire again.

'Don't you have your key?' she shouts.

'Yes! But I can't cross your threshold uninvited!' Teen Vamp shouts back.

'In which case...!' says the landlady... and leaves him there till morning.

House of Commons

We're pagans, but like all pagans, that isn't all we do or all that we are. Trevor has a background in IT: he was a software consultant for years, working across Europe. I worked in international education and lived in Central Asia. We have professional and academic connections. We go horse-racing. Trevor is working on a degree in Classics and History. I'm a science-fiction writer as well as a witchcraft shop owner. Pagans tend to do a lot of things, and we are no exception.

We went up to London last night as part of the Magdalene Association. I did my doctorate (in history and philosophy of science) at Cambridge, ending up at Magdalene – which, let's just say, wasn't really the ideal match for a left-wing feminist. But I retain an affection for my old college, which holds regular functions and we occasionally attend.

This one was a dinner at the House of Commons, so we closed the shops early and caught the train up to town. Trevor went out and bought a black tie, but got the car clamped while doing so – it must be the most expensive bow tie ever. We got to the House early, and had a wander around the public bits, which are always spectacular – one day I'm going to write a story about that central lobby with all the magnificent mosaic representations of the British saints. We then took ourselves off to the river terrace for a bit before going into dinner – this particular function was sponsored by Henry Bellingham, an alumnus of the college, who is MP for NW Norfolk (I think) and at the time of writing, Shadow Minister for justice. He's a Tory. T and I ended up sitting opposite the MPs who were present and Bellingham seemed pleasant, sharp and down to earth, which makes a nice change for a politician. I have since looked up his voting record and find that he has asked pertinent questions about increasing the number of female entrepreneurs, funding for rape crisis centres and environmental technology, so go him even if he is a Conservative. Magdalene doesn't turn out many Labour politicians.

We were seated opposite one Adam Holloway, who turns out to be slightly younger than myself and is also an MP. He's done some interesting stuff (he was in the Grenadier Guards, and was a war correspondent in Bosnia – he's also done a lot of investigative reporting into, e.g., the psychiatric treatment of schizophrenia). He rather blotted his copybook by admitting that he was also the founder of Black October, which sounds like a Marxist guerrilla movement, but was actually a group at Magdalene when I joined the college, in protest at the admission of (gasp!) women students. I was part of the first intake and I guess must have been one of the first female postgraduates (since 1428).

Needless to say all the elderly dons were in favour of the presence of girls in their hallowed halls (more for the promise of mini-skirts than innate feminism, one suspects) and all the young whippersnappers objected. Holloway did, however, apologise, and so I should think. Some kudos must go to much of the association for not immediately assuming that Trevor was the alumnus instead of me (the couple who did so also apologised).

The other person we were with turns out to have been de-selected (for telling the truth about his party's spending cuts, apparently – it's absolutely typical of the political establishment to sack someone for being honest). He was a very charming man. I always note how people treat the waiting staff at these things and all the politicians present were good in that regard (okay, maybe they just don't want the staff to spit in the soup, but at least it shows some manners). My actual neighbour was an economist, but we didn't go much into that because he said, rightly, that it was just too depressing.

One of the MPs said that it had been an 'interesting' day in the House and that after 24 hours of Peter Mandelson and Russian oligarchs it was 'nice to spend an evening with normal people.' I refrained, at that point, from telling him exactly what it was that we did for a living, but perhaps it wouldn't have mattered.

Dinner itself was smoked salmon, duck in a pastry and ceps parcel, and pear tart. The wine was excellent. We had to bolt for the train at 10 pm but just as we were about to do so, the division bell went and things more or less broke up anyway.

Next day, someone asked Trevor why on earth he'd wanted to go to the House of Commons. 'Let me think,' he replied. 'It's not at all like Glastonbury, is it? It's a weird, enclosed community governed by its own strange rituals, where everyone wears peculiar clothes and drinks a lot – oh wait.'

Spinning, Weaving, Dyeing
Our friend P has spent most of the day attacking my shrubbery with a chainsaw, to great effect.

More delicately, the autumn is always a time for study and I have started my spinning, weaving and dyeing course again, at the Adult Learning Centre in Wells. I'm not the most gifted person when it comes to handicrafts – anything I sew ends up with three sleeves, and that's just the skirts – but to my surprise, I have turned out to be good at spinning and reasonably adept at weaving as well. I spin on a wheel bought from an elderly lady in Bath who sadly broke her arm and had to give up the practice, rather than a spindle. Something about the rhythmic quality of the practice makes me understand what Morgaine in Marion

Zimmer Bradley's *The Mists Of Avalon* means when she speaks of spinning sending her into a trance: it's almost hypnotic.

In addition to this, I have made soup and a game stew with ceps and gone into town to meet up with Trevor, who has been compering the local psychic fair all day.

We also met Professor Searl, inventor of an alleged anti-gravity device (he prefers 'inverse gravity'), who was supposed to be staying with us this week. This completely freaked me out as I studied Searl's work at university, during a foray into artificial intelligence, and the possibility of having one of the most eminent philosophers of mind of his generation to stay has made me realize how much of the philosophy of mind I can't remember.

The day before, I realized he is a different Searl. Whew.

The professor had to delay his trip until today, but having finally appeared, turns out to be a delightful elderly gentleman in full military uniform. I assumed this was from the RAF until I got a closer look at it, and it turns out to be an Inverse Gravity Device Pilot's uniform, complete with wings. Wow! And he has a beautiful blonde assistant (our mutual friend D).

I feel as though I'm living in a Gerry Anderson cartoon. Even Glastonbury hasn't quite known how to take the Professor.

Welcome to Fairyland

When I first set eyes on Glastonbury – the strange little hump of the Tor rising out of the Levels, seen from the Mendip edge – I was enchanted. Okay, I *was* only twelve: we were driving from Gloucester down to a family holiday in Lyme Regis. I knew all about Glastonbury, being the kind of child who read a lot of stories about King Arthur, and the feeling of wonder that came over me when I stood in front of the legendary graves in the Abbey is something that I've rarely experienced since. Even at 12, I knew that the graves were highly unlikely to be those of Arthur and his Queen; that they were, most probably, an early scam organized by an ailing Abbey who needed to rustle up funds.

Even so, the thought that this, the ground I was standing on, was Avalon itself had a massive impact on me and that impact has never really gone away.

I suppose that's what 'enchantment' means.

I didn't return to Glastonbury until thirteen years later, when I was in my mid-twenties. I wasn't the sort of student who headed off to the Festival every summer (I still haven't been, although I have been on site at Pilton in the periods before and after it all kicks off). I don't like crowds and I can't stand camping, which rather puts the mockers on attending one of the world' largest rock festivals. (*She doesn't like camping because there's nowhere to plug in the hairdryer*) But as I've said elsewhere in this Diary, my late partner Charles had friends who at that time ran the Assembly Rooms and when we'd been going out for a few months, the time came around for a visit.

It was spring – around Easter, and as chilly and pale as that time of year can often be. We came up the A37, through Pilton, and as the Tor grew in the distance I once more felt as I had when I'd first seen it as a child. By then, I'd read, and loved, *The Mists Of Avalon*, a book which inspires equal affection and rage in residents of Glastonbury – sometimes in the same breath. The orchards under the Tor were a lacy mass of delicate blossom, and I thought of Morgaine, riding in through the mists.

Of course, I loved it. I loved all the old hippy ways that were still extant in the town then (still are, to some degree, although I must say that a true sign of age is that now they annoy me as much as anything else). People playing guitars on the slopes of the Tor. Arty parties in local bookshops. And of course, the weird little shops. I think The Goddess and the Green Man was there then, in the Glastonbury Experience courtyard (known untactfully as the Ghastly Experience to many of the then-residents). If I recall correctly, and I may not, what is now the Blue Note cafe was run by a pair of women known to our friends as the Tofu Maidens. All the food was brown and lumpy and it might have been good for you, but it didn't look like it was.

The George and Pilgrim was much the same, but it's difficult to alter a listed and loved building. We used to drink there a lot, and also in the Beckett's up the High Street, and in the Rifleman's Arms. In fact, it's hard to think of a pub we didn't drink in, due to our friend C's habit of upsetting people and getting banned. He was banned from the Rifleman's, which is quite a feat, and spent someone's birthday sitting in a tree just behind the pub's car park, being passed pints until the landlady realized what was happening and became incandescent with rage. I estimate C has probably been banned consecutively from every pub in Glastonbury and eventually he moved to Babcary, from which he cycled to and fro. (He was briefly banned from the Red Lion in Babcary as well, for setting the dog on a yuppie at Christmas and for parking the tractor in their car park).

Over the next fifteen years, and after Charles died, I visited the town about twice a year. We developed the habit of going just before Christmas, on the way from Brighton to my parents in Gloucester. And we quite often went down in the summer, for a succession of birthday parties. There were occasional spring and autumn visits as well, so I got to know the town in all its moods, from the apple blossom and thin winds of spring, to the hazy, flower-filled summers, the mists of autumn and the icy glassy fields of winter.

Everyone said: *don't ever live here. You know what it does.*

I did know. I loved Glastonbury, but I loved visiting it. I had no intention of ever moving here, until, as I have related, I met Trevor. And even then I was very wary – not of my new relationship, which has always felt right, but of the town itself. I'd seen what it could do to people. I knew about the Glastonbury Experience, when in your first few years of residence, the town seems to take what you most fear and hold up a wicked, mocking mirror that, like a hippy Alice, you must pass through or perish.

I thought I'd been through a lot. I wondered what the hell else was on the way.

What the Glastonbury Experience put us through, in the

space of a couple of years, was this:

– serious injuries – 1 (me: four days in hospital in Taunton with a ruptured spleen, a torn kidney and a broken rib after a fall from our horse)

– throat cancer (Trevor)

– numerous deaths of family and friends

– an employee who couldn't take what she saw in that mirror and was claimed by madness (see later on in the diary)

– the threat of bankruptcy

...And more besides, which I won't go into. But things did remain intact, including our relationships, with one another and with our families.

However, Glastonbury being what it is, we get a lot of new people in town. Quite a lot of them also know about the Experience and are prepared for it, as far as one can be. Some people are convinced they can handle it and they're the ones who usually cop it big-time: sectioning under the Mental Health Act, addiction, loss of work or homes. Some have the humility to doubt, and they usually get off relatively lightly (although I aimed at humility and still copped it).

When the Pilgrim Centre ran a workshop on the Experience, I gave a talk on it, and so did a couple of other long term Glastonbury residents. A young man of Scandinavian extraction stood up at the end and, with great passion, announced that he was such an elevated and open soul that he planned to move here and open his heart. Thus, he would avoid the Experience. All it took, he said, was a willingness to go with the flow and truly Trust.

I have not seen him from that day to this.

The Experience seems, also, to depend to some degree on the extent to which you have to engage with the place. Many people survive and, rather ruefully, thrive. They still rub their psychic bruises, though.

The ones whom Glastonbury really chews up and spits out (although a few hang on, usually in a continually unstable state) are those who come to town convinced that they will be the Next Big Thing. They're going to really shake the place up. They're a High Priest, or a High Priestess, or an Archdruid. They've usually got some kind of connection with Atlantis. Quite often, they're convinced that they're channelling Arthur, or Morgaine Le Fay, or occasionally Guinevere. Quite often, too, they believe themselves to be walk-ins: those who have been overtaken by a fairy or an alien consciousness. We once suffered a very difficult dinner in which Trevor's neighbour informed him that she hailed from the Pleiades and – despite being female and young – had been on the *Eldridge* at the time of the Philadelphia Experiment (I think there is now general agreement that this was a degaussing experiment designed to make the boat invisible to enemy radar, not invisible to *everything*).

Call me psychic, but I just *knew* Trevor was going to say something unfortunate and that's when I suddenly remembered a hitherto-unmentioned, yet pressing, prior engagement. As they say, we made our excuses and left.

Dealing with this kind of thing is part of the pagan party line. It's not the done thing to criticize other people's beliefs: this is regarded as judgmental. Damn right! It *is* judgmental. If you want to get philosophically technical, paganism espouses a relativist ontology. Marx was right: when the church fails, people don't believe in nothing – they believe in anything. But the problem is, we all *are* judgmental, at least internally. We might be too polite to say things in our 'out loud' voice, but we're certainly thinking 'God, that's just nuts.' Unless you're completely vacuous, there's always going to be a point at which you start drawing the boundaries between what you believe and what you just can't stomach. For example, a lot of people I know think David Icke makes some valid points about the political process but they simply can't get past the 12 foot lizard thing.

Most of the time, those who cleave to what I will intolerantly refer to as the madder beliefs are harmless. Occasionally, they're arrogant and that's where problems start. A very wise Cornish pagan recently pointed me in the direction of an article in the online pagan magazine Witchvox which talks about dysfunctional paganism. Rather than just believing what people say, the authors suggests, take a look at their lives. It's all very well for folk to claim to be Enlightened Beings, but there's not much point in that if they're sliding from disastrous relationship to disastrous relationship, don't speak to their families, can't hold down a job and have a drugs problem. Who in their right mind is going to listen to anything someone like that has to say? Yes, we all have crises occasionally. No one lives a life of impeccable perfection. But the Craft, or Druidry, or whatever you practice, should enable you to overcome your problems, not to play the perpetual victim.

Specific cases come to mind. There's the High Priestess who ran into us in a restaurant a few nights after our friend E's mother had unexpectedly died. E (not a High Priestess) ended up having to prop up the HP as she collapsed in a drunken heap, mourning the death of her sister several years previously. Not good enough and yes, I am judgmental.

There's the individual whose name on the leaked BNP mailing list specifies that they are a witch, with a note alongside saying that it would be 'embarrassing' if their fascist political allegiances were to be made public. I'll say.

There's the woman who's 'been a witch for twenty years' whom Trevor had to fire in the very early days of Witchcraft Ltd, who has a criminal record for theft, deals in class A drugs, and has a penchant for telling the world about her experiences at fetish clubs. As a friend of hers remarked, she's done one year of witchcraft twenty times and still hasn't learned anything.

And then there are all the fractured covens, the spats and spits on mailing lists and forums, the schisms in tiny little Druidic groups, the hexing wars (we've had blood smeared over the door of the shop – all you'd need to do for a prosecution would be to send it to a lab for DNA testing), the semi-literate, pompous outpourings – all the dirty secrets that paganism likes to pretend doesn't exist. They call it 'Bitchcraft' for a reason.

Not good enough. And if that means I'm judgmental, then I'm happy to be so.

Only in Glastonbury…

Only in Glastonbury would you get a Charity event called in by the Town Crier, followed by the worshipful Mayor of the town in full regalia playing the saxophone.

Right outside the Cat and Cauldron in the Market Place.

Audience: four, plus two dogs.

Only in Glastonbury would you then, not five minutes later, stand in respect for a funeral cortege – one old banger with the grieving contacts – followed by the coffin – an eco-cardboard job – in a specifically designed – MOTOR-CYCLE SIDECAR!

The Mists of Avalon

When a lot of people think of Glastonbury, they think of Marion Zimmer Bradley's famous novel *The Mists Of Avalon*. I read it as a young woman, and loved it, but alas, it bears no relationship to the historical Glastonbury – this is, I suppose, why Bradley made Avalon a kind of parallel universe, with its stones on top of the Tor instead of the tower. We have no evidence of human occupation of the island before about the 8th century, and there's no evidence at all of groups of Goddess-worshipping priestesses anywhere in the British Isles before 1880 (with the exception of a couple of Roman era Iseums, granted). The 'Fortunate Isles' to which the wounded Arthur is taken are first mentioned in the works of Isidore of Seville and are the Canaries – the Hesperides, land of 'golden apples' (there are still golden-globed fruit on the trees of the Canaries. They're called oranges). This has led to irreverent speculation in my social circle that Arthur got whisked off to a kind of Avalonian Club Med. It's here that the Nine Morgens are first mentioned; nothing to do with Glastonbury at all until Isidore's story is lifted by Geoffrey of Monmouth to form part of the British legend of Avalon.

Geoffrey's Morgan is probably based on Medea or Circe, with a Celtic twist given by her name, a version of the Morrigan.

However, as an occult novel, *Mists* is one of the most influential of the last fifty years. I never got on as well with its precursor or its sequels, but am now re-reading them more or less in sequence and find that I am considerably more engaged with the series as a whole, basically because, if read in sequence, it becomes a lot easier to follow the series of reincarnations which these books are basically about: all the books are more or less about four people, three women and one man. I read Marion Zimmer Bradley's *The Fall Of Atlantis* before I read *Mists*, and didn't realise that these are part of the same story.

I still think that she tapped into something with *Mists* that isn't quite there with the other books, however. (I find it interesting that the current priestess course here in Glastonbury seems to have started off by drawing an awful lot from the novel, but I'm not sure if that's either intentional – I suspect it might not be – or simply because so many of the ideas in the book seem to have seeped out into the esoteric zeitgeist. And please note, I'm not knocking the course – I am a supporter of the Goddess Temple here in town and consider it a good thing). Or did both tap into something else? Possibly so.

What I have found interesting, however, is a connection which I haven't seen anywhere before. That's the link between *Mists* and Dion Fortune's *The Sea Priestess*. In the Fortune novel, written in 1938, the central character is of course Vivian Le Fay Morgan – apparently ageless, mysterious, and with a surprisingly strong sense of humour. The background to the story is Atlantean and a lot of the terms that subsequently turn up in the Avalon series emanate from this earlier novel: the place names (the river Naradek, for instance, which I can't find anywhere else, though it may be an element of mystery school tradition – I know Dolores Ashcroft-Nowicki does workshops on Atlantean magic), and the magic itself. I'd imagine that MZB used these deliberately as either a homage, or because she felt that Fortune was onto something (DF claimed that she channelled a lot, and one may take this on board or not depending on one's spiritual views). But the parallels between the books are striking and worth further exploration.

I am also intrigued by the parallels between a writer who starts a story about two sisters (the reincarnatory cycle is kicked off with Domaris and Deoris), who then hands over the rights to the series to her sister-in-law, who is herself a practicing priestess.

I recently watched the made-for-video version of the story and was more than somewhat taken aback when the mists parted to reveal an enormous Grecian temple rather than our little hill.

Still, there's historical truth and there's poetic truth, and Bradley's Avalon is a lovely image. And in winter, when the mists rise up off the Levels, you can reach the bottom of Northload Street and suddenly pass through into bright sunshine – it's due to the temperature differential between a slightly raised area of ground and the lower flat land of the wet Levels.

So the Mists do exist, and it would be nice to think that maybe, just maybe, one day you'll see them part and you'll pass through, not into Northload St, but into that bluerobed community of women.

Psychic Investigation at the White Spring

Via Glastonbury Radio, we got invited to a psychic investigation last night in the White Spring, some of which was filmed, and which will probably form the basis of a Glastonbury TV inaugural broadcast.

For those who don't know, the White Spring is an actual spring – opposite the red chalybeate spring of the Chalice Well – that is highly calcium-bearing. It was turned into a Victorian pumping station to provide the town with fresh water after a cholera outbreak, except that the calcium furred up the pipes in no time at all and rendered it useless, exactly like a lime-scaled kettle. It's now been bought by a friend of ours and given to the town as a shrine. It has, in contemporary Glastonbury legend, become associated with Gwyn ap Nudd, leader of the Wild Hunt and king of the fairies in legends from Elizabethan times onward. He may or may not be a Celtic god of the dead. But he's supposed to live under the Tor, and the White Spring is on the side of the hill. A couple of months ago, some people did a ritual to unblock the doorway so that Gwyn was free to wander about.

Trevor spent several hours locked in there last year when he had the throat cancer, having a word with the dodgy old god. For the purposes of this discussion, I am treating Gwyn as though he is in some manner a real entity.

There were about a dozen people there: ourselves, Ross and his partner from the radio station, the staff of the spring, and four clairvoyants. We were split into two teams and initially had to form two circles at each side of the spring, and see what we picked up. The first one, in front of a shrine to the Black Madonna, was fairly standard – people getting bits and pieces of what may or may not have been information, impressions, etc.

Trevor felt very faint halfway through and had to sit down. When we went to the other side of the spring, however, things got more dramatic. This is the side that is supposed to be the entrance to the underneath of the Tor – author Geoffrey Ashe says it's actually a series of rooms connected to the pumping station, but it may lead into caves (there are a lot of them around here).

Again, the clairvoyants got bits and pieces of stuff. Halfway through, one of them, Mike, apologised to Trevor and said that he was getting a strong message to put his hands round Trevor's throat – not to strangle him, but just to place his hands there. He did this for several minutes then came back into the circle. Then Helen asked Mike a question and he didn't answer. She asked again. Still no reply. He had, in fact, gone completely into trance. She started asking whatever had done it if it could talk to us, but there was no response, so I said 'Can you show us?' and at that, Mike pitched straight forward – didn't buckle at the knees, just fell, as if he'd been pole-axed. Fortunately he fell on Trevor, who was opposite and probably the one person who could take Mike's weight.

We got him into a chair and he started coming round. He was very groggy for a bit and then said that, from his point of view, the wall opened up, he fell through it and into the gaping maw of a huge bear on the other side.

At this point Trevor turned round and said, 'Gwyn? BASKET!'

It turns out that Mike is a straight clairvoyant, by which I mean that he doesn't work with any one tradition, apart from spiritualist churches, and he didn't know much about the local folklore. We explained all the local mythology about Gwyn to him and Mike said that he'd been given, in some manner, a message for Trevor: that the 'debt had been paid in full'. He didn't know about the throat cancer. I told him that if he had been contacted by, basically, the king of the fairies, he was not to take any nonsense and this was immediately backed up by the two WS staff members, who said that Gwyn is known for playing with people and you have to stand up to him/it. Gwyn isn't associated with bears as far as I know, however, although King Arthur legendarily is, and he has associations with Glastonbury for obvious reasons.

I have to say that Mike does not, apart from whatever gifts he might have, strike me as a flaky person, and he didn't treat any of this as though it was particularly disturbing. And all of this is subject to an entirely rational explanation.

Whatever the psychological mechanisms at work, however, Trevor closed Gwyn's door again, quietly and when no one else was looking.

We left at midnight.

Ouija

Normally, our customers know what they're doing. Samhain seems to bring out the ones who don't, however. Today, I had the following conversation:

Bloke: 'Isn't witchcraft illegal?'

Me: 'Actually, no. Not since the 50s.' [inner voice: *Yes! That's why we have an entire town devoted to it in full public view!*]

Bloke: 'So do you sell ouija boards?'

Me: 'Yes. Do you know what you're doing?'

Bloke: 'Er, no.'

Me: 'Then I'm not selling you one.'

Bloke: [slightly flummoxed] 'Is it that dangerous, then?'

Me: 'They're for contacting the dead.' [inner voice: *who almost certainly don't want to be bothered with you*]. 'They're not a toy.'

He went away slightly nonplussed, but at least better informed.

Ghost Hunt

We're spending this evening in the office, with a ghost hunt. Trevor and I spent yesterday evening making Hallowe'en cookies (Trevor decorated lots of little cat cookies with an icing spot under the tail before I realised what he was doing) and carving a pumpkin for the shop. The town is inundated with people.

Later. I'm sitting in a haunted 200 year old building which houses a witchcraft shop, on Hallowe'en, in the ancient Isle of Avalon, with a ghost hunt going on around me, and I'm looking up pumpkin stencils on the internet. It might be possible to become too blase.

Lock-in

I just had to confess – I have been pricing things up all morning and the ceramic hares were in danger of toppling off the mountain, so I took them up to Liz at the Magick Box.

I locked Bear [*our dog – Ed*] inside and left the *Back in 5 Minutes* sign. When I got back in with my lunch bag, Bear was very pleased to see me. And so was the very pretty German Lady who had been trying dresses on in the back of the shop...

Ooops!

She loved the idea so much she stayed for another half an

hour, and then gave us the biggest sale of the day – 2 beautiful velvet dresses, which she showed off to me.

Those particular dresses only arrived yesterday, so they continue the long tradition of last thing in the shop is the first thing sold!

Be that as it may, I did give the lady a small discount and a free gift to compensate for her trauma, and then Liz confessed to having done the same thing a while back, so we are evens. Liz said, 'perhaps there is a lesson there – lock them in and they spend.'

November

Witchfest

A 'must' on the pagan calendar for the last few years has been Witchfest: the big pagan conference held in Croydon. We try to get to this every year.

On this occasion, we drove down to Surrey on Friday night – an uneventful trip that dropped us in Dorking at an excellent Thai restaurant at 8 p.m., and subsequently in Reigate with our hostess. This is an old friend of mine, who is not a pagan, but a member of a High Church branch of the C of E. She's very tolerant of having the heathen show up with all their devilish works stuffed into the back of a Jeep.

On Saturday morning, we drove to the venue and unloaded, but were obliged to move the car for a pack of wolves, which is not normally something that happens to you in Croydon. These are supplied by one of the wolf conservation trusts – in previous years, people have been allowed into the pen to sit with them, but these are European wolves, apparently, and not entirely safe. One of them gave me an old, cold stare. Was she communicating a mystical message from the animal kingdom? Was she suggesting that I might adopt her as a totem?

I think she saw me as lunch.

Having shifted the car, we set up in fairly good time and spent the next 10 hours selling stuff. Witchfest was quieter than in previous years, but still hosted several thousand people, so it was a busy day. Our friend and assistant Elaine and I managed to sneak off to hear Ronald Hutton lecture on dragons, but due to an organisational failure on the part of someone in charge, what we got was a very dramatic man talking about ghosts on the Isle of Wight instead.

Witchfest sounds like fun and it was, but the loading and unloading process was exhausting. We were ready for a pint at the end of it, and noodles at the very good Asian café around the corner.

Carnival

We did the shop window of the Magick Box tonight – following the Samhain window, I did one that related to the forthcoming Witches' Ball. It features a model in a ball gown and the dummy known to us as Antlered Man, and to the staff as Becks, due to his resemblance to a certain football personality. AM has, duh, antlers, which had to be sawed down so that he could fit in the window, and he only just does. Trevor was therefore to be seen cursing heavily and apparently embracing a half-naked mulleted bloke with stag's horns in the shop window at 7 p.m. this evening. (A woman had previously seen me carrying Antlered Man's torso up the High St: 'Only in Glastonbury,' she said).

In New Orleans or Rio, 'carnival' means fabulous costumes, samba music, flowers and fireworks. Well, we've got the fireworks. In Somerset, Carnival means massive floats, built on low loaders and pulled by John Deere tractors with enormous wheels. Some of them are so big that they only just fit through the streets of the little Somerset towns. Glastonbury is no exception: for our town, Carnival is one of the biggest trading days of the year. I regret to relate that apart from this, neither Trevor or myself can stand it. When I moved here, I thought it would be like the lovely Winter Solstice parades they held in Brighton, with floating paper animals and children in imaginative costumes. But it's not. All the floats are based on Disney characters or popular culture and the whole thing betrays a staggering lack of imagination, in my admittedly snobbish view. But a lot of people love it and just because it's not to my taste is no reason why other people shouldn't enjoy it.

We spent the day serving customers, then made a break for it at six, driving at speed towards a large crowd of carnival-goers who were obliged to leap out of the way.

Then, round the back roads (the main roads are cordoned off), we came to a road block.

'Get out of the car! Take it down! Don't argue!' Trevor barked, as though we'd just staged a bank heist. Rather to my own surprise, I did what he said and the getaway vehicle surged through. I wrestled the barrier back into position, consumed by guilt. I always feel guilty when I see a policeman, even if I haven't done anything, let alone when I actually have.

We were not arrested but headed towards Meare in a squeal of tyres and angst. I gather Carnival went well.

Folklore Society

I went up to London today for the Katharine Briggs Memorial Lecture at the Warburg Institute, home to the Folklore Society, of which I am a member. Reaching town about 3 p.m., I went to the Atlantis bookshop first (I found a 19th century edition of a book on West Country legends). Then I had something called Bibimbap in a Korean cafe – I've never come across this before, despite having been to Korea (it turns out to be greens, noodles, rice, meat, beansprouts and a fried egg in a bowl).

Prior to the memorial lecture, Prof Sidney Brandes from Berkeley gave a talk on the Mexican Day of the Dead, including an analysis of why Mexicans are opposed to Hallowe'en (nasty imperialist festival taking over their own 'homegrown' one, even though both come from the same source – there's very little evidence, apparently, that the Day of the Dead is pre-Spanish, rather as there's very little evidence for Samhain actually being an ancient Celtic festival of the dead and the start of the new year, as we saw).

I outed myself during the questions as a proprietor of a witchcraft shop, which in a company of mainly academic anthropologists caused much hilarity – in a nice way. Our window was generally acclaimed this year, possibly because it featured less plastic and an actual pumpkin – that, ahem, ancient Celtic vegetable.

Dr Jacqueline Simpson then gave the memorial lecture itself – she is a formidable woman with a slight French accent and a very forthright delivery. Along with co-author Jennifer Westwood, she wrote folklore book *The Lore Of The Land*, which I've been using for our radio show for the last couple of years. Simpson's account of dealing with her publisher caused a massive collective wince, like a kind of Mexican wave, to run through her audience on several occasions.

'And when our editor took us out to dinner, 'e said, 'It is wonderful that you are both still speaking! Usually when we have two authors, they fall out before the book is finished!' We did not like to say, but the only *raison* we were still speaking that we both wanted to murder *'im*!'

There was a disagreement about the formatting of footnotes, apparently.

Erection and staff

It's a hard, bright autumn day with the sun going down over the Severn Sea and all the lights coming on in the High Street. We've had wonderful sunsets lately. If you had been in the Magick Box

yesterday, you'd have heard the following conversation between me and a customer in California: 'No – we have one with a staff and no erection, and a sitting-down one with an erection and no staff. Yes, both of them have horns.'

This is the trouble when you sell statues of the Horned God.

Staff Problems

We have staff problems. When we got back from a trip yesterday, we found a bunch of amateur models in Witchcraft, choosing clothes for today's fashion show at the Assembly Rooms. There was also a palpable Atmosphere, emanating from my employee and lodger.

Today, one of our non-gossipy friends informed me that Lodger spent most of yesterday in a loud, and continual, bitching session aimed at myself and Trevor, in front of customers, about – well, everything.

Lodger lived at our place rent free for 4 months while the council sorted out her housing benefit, and paid nothing for two years in heating, lighting or water. It was our decision, because she was on her uppers and couldn't afford it, and I'll take responsibility for that – although in retrospect, she always seemed to have enough money for clothes, laptops, jewellery and a huge tattoo. I gave her notice a month ago (she was already looking at other places) for the end of March.

Apparently, however, we 'think more of things than we do people' and have been callous and unfair. She has also been telling people that we have been neglecting Trevor's horse, who is elderly, unwell, and under the care of the vet, who has been running tests. Apparently it has not occurred to her to check with the vet.

I intend to fire her and rescind her notice for the end of December at the latest.

I'm sorry it's come to this. I feel, at the end of the day, that we cannot be the family whom Lodger so wants and whom she has alienated (she has two daughters, who have told her they don't want anything to do with her). But we have our own families and she's an adult woman, who continually tells those around her how much more capable she is than anyone else. I suppose she will now have to live with that contention.

The Witches' Ball

On Thursday night, we hosted the shops' first music gig: a Witches' Ball in Glastonbury. This was a success – we had a buffet supper supplied by the local Indian restaurant, live music (Damh the Bard) and a Samhain ritual, which was done along American pagan lines by a friend (more theatrical than the Brits, who tend to mumble).

Halfway through the ritual, which was carefully choreographed to music, I became aware of a slight hiatus. Trevor stepped in and talked everyone through the next bit and I thought no more of it until we finished and a furious and weeping High Priestess informed me that she'd gone to see why the sound engineer hadn't cued in the next phase of music, and found he'd passed out face-down on the sound board. She brought him round but remains underwhelmed. Apparently he'd 'entered a trance state.'

When you do rituals, especially big public ones, you've got to be prepared for something to go wrong. It always does.

Apart from this, the Ball went without a hitch and the 60 or so folk who turned up all said they had a great time.

Fired

I saw Lodger yesterday outside the shop and mercifully – despite being busy all day – there were no customers during the period in which I fired her. This was not an easy thing to do and I didn't like having to do it. Lodger clearly did not understand that there's a problem and a suspicion that has been brewing for some time is now confirmed: she doesn't actually seem to remember what she said or that she said anything. Either that or she's just denying it, but somehow, I think she genuinely believes it. Comments in recent weeks that other people have made about her keep coming back to 'manic', 'hyper' and 'can't stop talking.' I have considered that she might be bipolar and undiagnosed, but she doesn't seem depressive enough. I don't know enough about it and I also don't want to go down the road of 'she disagrees with me therefore she

MUST be mad', because I think that's a bit peculiar on my part, frankly.

Anyway, I went to my Druidic group in Bristol last night. They know me well and they also know Lodger – she was part of the wider group years ago and lived with some close friends of my group 'leader.' I don't know what the previous problems were – it's not a gossipy set – but warning bells were rung a year or so ago when I met Lodger's former landlady and she paled on sight of Lodger and said, 'Oh God, I hope she doesn't want to come and live with us again.'

Dartmoor

Because we are so busy, it's difficult to get time off to do workshops – the ones you're reading about in this diary took place over 3 to 4 years. But Carolyn Hillyer's workshops are something I've wanted to do for a long time, and so I managed to book some time off.

I drove down on Friday afternoon, arriving just before dusk – a very impressive stretch of country under a windswept sky, incredibly bleak. On arriving, the Jeep promptly got stuck in the mud, necessitating the use of the 4 wheel drive. We had dinner and then I took several women up to where we were staying – because this was a big group and the cottage has limited space, we were at a neighbouring farm instead, where they have facilities for walkers.

On Saturday, I went for a short walk on the moor, but it rained, so I did not spend long out there. However, we were due to spend most of the day inside, either in circle in the main room, or in Carolyn's roundhouse.

We did various practical things, including carving a spool (for spinning) out of hazel, and a long vigil session in the roundhouse on Saturday night, which involved a ritual. Saturday was the silent day, and we were asked not to speak except to relay practical information. Needless to say this cracked the minute we got in the car, but we did try. Sunday was a similar day in terms of activities, but the weather was even fouler, so not much time outside...

It being so close to Samhain, the workshop was all about death. The other thing we made, apart from the spool, was a grave totem – basically, a thing like a dead baby, out of stones and fleece and wrappings. I realise that this may sound very macabre, but a lot of the women found it helpful to externalise and ritualise what they'd been through. I've had a tough time over the last few years, but some of the women there had been through equal amounts of awfulness.

I won't say too much about the roundhouse ritual, because this might spoil it for people who go on to do the workshop (for the record, there is little that is secret about many esoteric traditions, but because it is an experiential path, it's more helpful to do things without prior knowledge). But my impressions – darkness, ochre, fire, and drumming.

I have huge respect for Carolyn Hillyer. I think she is one of the most remarkable women I know, as well as one of the nicest, and the bar was pretty high to start with.

After this, I joined some of the women who were staying overnight for dinner at the Warren House Inn, which is up on the high moor – a lovely place dating from the mid 19th century, when it replaced a 800 year old pub which had finally fallen down. Tiled floor, log fires at both ends of the room, mulled wine and rabbit pie. Then I drove home, arriving an hour and a half later – not bad from the middle of the moor.

Ireland

Off to Ireland on a mission. We've been promising for some time to travel over to Meath and collect some ritual gear belonging to the late witch and journalist Stewart Farrar, which his widow is very kindly donating to the Museum of Witchcraft in Boscastle.

There was a slight panic on Monday as some ferries were cancelled due to the high winds, but when I phoned, it turned out that this was from Holyhead in the north.

It was a cold, clear day. We drove down to Wales early and got to Pembroke Dock around midday, to sit in the queue for the boat for an hour or so. We spent our time on the *Isle of Inishmore* in the bar at the prow, reading, writing (in my case) and watching the long span of Milford Haven, with its oil refineries and huge foreign tankers, unspool ahead before we reached the Irish Sea. A small quantity of Guinness was consumed. We had a snack in the restaurant. Irish boats are mainly crewed by Poles. I tried to buy soup with just the nice soda bread they had in the 'serve yourself' section rather than have the bread roll as well, but was informed in Soviet tones that 'roll is included in price.' *No roll* was not an option. I have long since learned not to argue with Slavic waiting staff, because one will simply lose. Then we went in the duty free and found a quite remarkable amount of tat, mostly relating to leprechauns, and 'traditional Irish craft wear,' which turned out to mean green and white football shirts. Actually, come to think of it...

Trevor spent his time reading Pete McCarthy's account of drinking around Ireland, *McCarthy's Bar*, and occasionally laughing so much that people looked at us strangely.

I like boats. There's more room than on trains and planes, and you can wander about and get fresh air. It being out of season and midweek, the ferry was very quiet and there were plenty of places to sit. There's also enough room for a laptop and one retains a cellphone signal all the way across: it just slides onto the Irish network when still in sight of Wales. Admittedly, the advantages of ferries are somewhat negated by their tendency to plunge up and down outside harbours for hours (Charles was once on an Irish ferry that spent seven hours doing this outside Dublin: even the crew were ill). I am not afflicted with sea sickness and like the plunging bit, but Trevor is slightly more sensitive. On the other hand, Trevor has most of his 'competent crew' qualification and has sailed yachts to France, whereas I have to ask which side the starboard is. Also, although the Irish Sea is, well, sea, the run through Milford Haven is interesting:

Napoleonic sea forts, towering pieces of industrial equipment, massive red cliffs and islands, including Skomer, where I spent a brief spell as an assistant volunteer wildlife warden in the mid 1990s, and Ramsey ('Garlic Island'), around which I have been on a much smaller boat to go seal watching. Further out, you can see the more horrific bits of the Pembrokeshire coast, like the Needles (self explanatory) and the Bitches (ditto). If I remember correctly, there is a twelve foot tide differential on one side of the Bitches and rather a lot of sunken ships underneath them.

We got into Rosslare four hours later (the *I of I* is not the faster catamaran that they used to have on this run and may still do, but in fact it isn't very far). The guest house is up on the cliffs. We were slightly horrified to read in one of the guesthouse books that a previous ferry had overshot the dock and flattened Wexford's new and extremely expensive lifeboat: I bet they were pleased.

We had dinner at a local pub, Culleton's. Irish pubs are much more like American bars than like British pubs, but none the worse for that.

On Wednesday morning we drove up to Meath, via the outskirts of Dublin, and arrived in Kells around lunchtime. Janet Farrar and Gavin Bone live in a fairly remote cottage, with an 800 year old well for water, and a megalithic circle in the walls of the house (it got cut up for the stone). Also seven cats, all of whom are delightful. So we spent the rest of Wednesday drinking tea and being sat on by cats, with a brief foray outside to admire the goats (Fanny the nanny recently got impregnated by a crazed, but evidently charismatic, wandering buck goat, who had to be shot for attacking a farmhand, and the result is the baby goat Pan).

Thursday saw more glorious weather. We woke up to a stiff frost and after a morning of driving on the previous day, did not feel like going far. Our hostess had to sort out a sore throat, as she had a film crew coming in to do some shooting. So Trevor and I went over to Slieve Na Cailleach (Hill of the Witches), where there is a massive Neolithic burial mound. It's a remarkable place – no one else was there, so we wandered around the mounds undisturbed. It was, however, freezing, so we went for lunch in a pub in Oldcastle (beef stew: the only thing on the menu. Our hostess in Wexford apparently tried to go vegan for a year, but failed), then drove back just before sunset. Trevor and Gavin had to go out in the evening to collect something, so Janet and I sat indoors and told stories. And were sat on some more by cats: Neelix (vast, ginger and white) fell in love with Trevor and pinned him to the sofa whenever he appeared, stout white arms wrapped around Trevor's neck, face buried in his beard, purring madly.

As I've said, the reason we went over was to collect some of Stewart Farrar's ritual equipment, which she was reluctant to entrust to a courier. So we'll be heading down to Cornwall soon to deliver it. We also got to look at some of Janet's archives – Stewart was evidently a great letter writer (as a journalist, this isn't surprising) and I went through his correspondence with Doreen Valiente: both of them tough-minded witches with a strong sense of humour. I wish Stewart and Doreen had got the recognition that Alex Sanders courted so assiduously, since in my opinion they were far better representatives of Wicca (I had a look through some of Sanders' training notes, which I doubt would pass muster today).

Janet and Stewart moved to Ireland about, I guess, thirty years ago, starting off in the west (where Janet was advised not to let her white horse graze on the shore, in case the sea god Mannanan Mac Lir took him away. The advice came from the local policeman).

Now, Janet is married to Gavin, and they live in Meath, where all the locals know they are witches (I think Stewart felt it was possibly better to be upfront about it). Janet said they've only had trouble once, from some American fundamentalists who came looking for Catholics to convert and decided to pick on the witches instead. But all the locals took the view that Janet and Gavin might be Brits and they might be witches, but they were *local* Brits and witches, *their* Brits and witches, and the people of Kells ran the fundamentalists out of town.

Janet got on very well with her previous landlord, and his son inherited the property – he's a typical Irish farmer, apparently, who goes on holiday to Lourdes to help with the sick. Last time he went, Janet asked him how it was and he said that it had been terrible – the Pope had shown up, and there were armed police in the streets. 'I tell you, Mrs Janet,' he said, 'We were all glad when the bastard went home to Italy.'

On Friday, we were due to return to Wexford, so we drove down via Tara. You realise how big a site it must have been in its heyday, though there isn't a lot to see now (it actually looks a bit like a golf course, although the Mound of the Hostages is pretty impressive).

There is, of course, a whacking big statue of St Patrick at the entrance to the site, looking especially grim, and a rather nice church. We also went down to a spring at the foot of the slope, my amateur archaeologist's eye assessing for suitability (easily defended, can see for miles, fresh water, etc).

Soon, you'll be able to get to Tara via a nice new motorway. It's actually on the other side of the existing road, and unlikely to be massively intrusive on the actual site: it's more the underlying historical stuff that its construction has already trashed and the corruption that it has exposed that are the worrying factors. But Tara itself is likely to remain peaceful on its green hill.

We drove back to Wexford via the Wicklow mountains, which are beautiful: we wanted more time to see them properly.

Arriving in the early evening, we went out to Horetown House for dinner – T stayed here several times for equestrian related stuff some years ago, when it was still officially a guest house (its owner refused hotel status because, she felt, she then wouldn't be able to 'mother the guests'.)

We caught the 8.45 out of Rosslare on Friday morning – another smooth trip, with a sea as calm as a millpond and the frost-white fields receding behind us. We got into Pembroke

Dock around midday and drove into Pembroke itself for lunch (bacon, cockles, laverbread (seaweed), in my case), before heading down to St Govan's chapel. This is a tiny, 6th century chapel in the cliffs (the building may date from the 11th century, or may be earlier). We returned to my cousins' farm via Carew Castle, by which time it was getting dark.

Most of my evening was spent at the hospital: my aunt is in there after a fall. She's on the mend, but she is 93. But it was good to see my family.

Yesterday, we had lunch in St David's, after a walk on Newgale Beach, then drove back to Somerset.

December

Winter Solstice

This is my favourite time of year. I loved Christmas as a child and that was in the days when we had the occasional white Christmas – and certainly heavy frosts. Now, we're still getting the frosts but not the snow and the Isle is beautiful in the winter months, truly the Isle of Glass. When you venture up onto the Tor, your breath steaming from your mouth like the breath of dragons, and stand on the short grass in the stillness and turn, you see the lands of the Levels stretching like a mirror beneath you and the lines of the rhynes running towards the sea, gleaming like mercury in the last of the light. The greater hills rise white in the distance: the Mendip edge, which is the first to catch any snow that does fall, the dragon-back hump of Brean Down, the angular shape of Brent Knoll. Beyond, the Quantocks, Exmoor, the Welsh hills stretch into shadow as the sun goes down in cold crimson fire and the lamp of the evening star flames up over the sea.

That's when you go down into the quiet cold town, your footsteps ringing on the frost, and the lights of the little Christmas trees are starring the street ahead of you and the candles on the tables in the George and Pilgrim are lighting the rising mist.

At this time of year, the Goddess Temple celebrates the winter goddesses: the white and icy ladies. We think of Freya, smiling behind her catskin hood, of Arianrhod of the Silver Wheel spinning destiny's skeins, of the ancient deities of the Siberian tundra, conjured out of the Great Cold.

Later, at the Solstice itself, the town is full of people heading for the Chalice Well under a hard white moon, the garden becomes a pale and ghostly place, and it's time for fires and stories and roasted chestnuts. Time to keep the dark at bay, time to keep the flame alight.

Recently, in the context of a kerfuffle over Xmas trees and menorahs at Seatac airport in Seattle, someone asked me about Yule/Solstice, and what we do for it. Getting united opinions out of pagans is like the legendary herding of cats, but this is what our household does:

– Christmas Tree: I've loved real trees in the house ever since I was a child, and some of my parents' decorations go back to before the War. We put up our own tree last night, which has Austrian wooden pine cones, brocade ribbon, small glass hanging birds and some cat angels. I don't think of it as a Solstice tree, but as a Christmas tree. We also have bunches of holly, ivy and mistletoe along the mantelpieces, and a decoration which my mother always made out of a couple of lampshades welded together: a round wire cage covered in fir and ivy, with apples hanging in the middle of it. I think these were originally Medieval.

I also send Christmas cards, although not usually with a Christian theme, it must be said. However, I did crack last year and send out some Russian cards with an angel and a cat sitting in a tree.

Around Solstice itself, Alban Arthuan ('the light of Arthur'), my Druidic group does a ritual, which is a fairly standard Druidic/Wiccan event: we call quarters for the four elements, and have some kind of role-play within it, usually around the theme of the sun's return, or the traditional battle between the Oak and the Holly King (Holly hands power over to Oak until the Summer Solstice). There are two rituals: one public, at Stanton Drew stone circle, and one private. They do not greatly differ apart from the number of people.

We usually do a household ritual on the evening of the Solstice itself, and these days I also light a candle somewhere (either in the local church or the local goddess temple) for my late partner, who died on Christmas Eve.

Some years ago, I did an evening Solstice Ceremony at Stonehenge, which was impressive: there was snow and a very clear sky, with a red sun in the west and a full moon rising in the east. Just before sunset, the whole plain turned as pink as a strawberry ice. Druids meet up at the dawn of the Solstice, which I will not be doing this year due to laziness.

We sometimes also go to the carol service at Gloucester Cathedral. I'm not very partisan about what I do, really: for me, all these fire festivals around this time of year merge into one, whatever their origins are supposed to be. It all comes from the same place and goes to it, in my opinion.

It does not make me at all happy that the last group to celebrate the Solstice in any great depth or number was the Nazi party. There was an interesting but repellent article about this in the *Fortean Times* this month: it was intended to replace Christmas as the new main holiday of the German state. My own Druidic group is run by an Anglo-Russian and an Anglo-Malaysian, neither of whom put any store in the notion of racial purity. At our celebrations, everyone is welcome, no matter what their nationality, race, or religion.

Winter Assembly

The weekend has been taken up by the Winter Assembly of the Order of Bards, Ovates and Druids, which always takes place at this time of year, and by our own group ritual. It's been a lot of fun, but very hectic. It was worth it for watching a Breton music band trying to organise line dancing for 60 people in a very small space.

The Winter Assembly is always somehow a more intimate affair than the Summer Assembly (these are the two main conclaves of the Order, plus the Mount Haemus lectures, which take place at the end of the summer every four years). The cold drives us all indoors and we take shelter in the pubs and cafes and, for the Assembly itself, in the Town Hall, where an immense heap of mistletoe fills the floor, its sticky white berries gleaming in the light of the chandelier.

The mistletoe is gathered by two members of the Order, from a farm close to Stanton Drew. The farmer is not a Druid – at least, not the robed and ritualizing kind with the golden sickle, like Getafix in the Asterix cartoon, or the kind like us. He's worked the land for years and he doesn't like to move far from it. He's quite happy for Druids to come onto his property and take the mistletoe out of his apple trees – although I've never asked whether they do so with that golden sickle. A steel-bladed knife is more likely, or a pair of secateurs.

The afternoon session of the Assembly is taken up by lectures, on various subjects. From the Assemblies I've learned about grimoires, about Arthur, about the history of the Order. Did you know, for example, that a group of modern Druids (1930s) died in Libya, gunned down by the Italian army for trying to defend a Sufi settlement?

(Overheard during the evening celebration: 'What are *you* doing these days?'

'Mainly, dressing up as a giant beetle and playing the ukelele.'

What's more, it's true. He does this for schools, apparently).

Women of the Celts

My friend Dr Kari Maund did a talk for OBOD on the subject of Arthurian magic – the stories of Cilhwch and Olwen, Gawain and the Green Knight, and Gawain and Ragnell. She was a little worried about giving this talk to OBOD – Kari is a Medieval historian specializing in early Medieval Wales and the role of Celtic women. There's a commonly accepted view – one that I myself held for many years – that Celtic women were much more emancipated than their Roman counterparts. Not so, says Kari. Most of the views of Celtic women as 'liberated' derive from Jean Markale, and he took an enormous span of history, from the

Dark Ages to 17th century Ireland, which is where most of the liberated bit comes from. But in Medieval Wales, women's roles were severely circumscribed: they were the property of the menfolk, little better than slaves, and all the tales of their magic in the original texts portray them as petty and spiteful. If you were an early Welsh warlord, Kari says, you'd no more think of consulting your wife on an issue than you would of consulting your (anachronistic) teapot.

The Druids – used to having Ronald Hutton debunk cherished illusions on a regular basis – take this well. Someone asks rather wistfully about ancient priestesses in the Celtic lands. No evidence, says Kari, firmly. Ah well.

The Rumour Mill

Meanwhile, I have caught up with the latest round of the town rumour mill, which I always publicise as much as possible in the hope of causing a stir. We generally read the wilder rumours out on the radio show, in order to give them maximum exposure. This time, according to public rumour, Trevor has £100,000 worth of gambling debts, but is attending Gamblers Anonymous, so that's all right.

This is so disastrously impressive that I am reluctant to set the record straight and make known the exact extent of those debts: 94p. He's hoping to win it back on Philadelphia Park over the next half hour, though.

Cleaning Up

Following a comment from a friend last night, I have been up into Lodger's flat – not something I normally do if she isn't there, because of the privacy issue, which I take seriously. I have now removed a lot – two bin bags full – of packets of past-sell-by-date, rotting meat, which she'd left on top of the bin, and some stuff which had been in the fridge for weeks. I sometimes find something ancient and bacterial at the back of our fridge so I can't cast huge stones at other people, but this was not pleasant.

I've arranged to have the whole place professionally cleaned when she leaves.

I also made the mistake of checking out Lodger's blog – I haven't done this before (didn't know she had one, in fact, and found it through Googling). It seems she was having a go at us as far back as 2006 – for example, for spending money on a workshop rather than spending it on her (perfectly reasonable and above minimum) wages. She was also apparently doing rituals to make us appreciate her more, rather than simply asking why we didn't, as the latter 'would have been manipulative.' Whereas doing covert magical rituals to alter someone else's emotions... isn't manipulative at all, apparently.

There was no mention that Trevor had just been diagnosed with cancer and hospitalised for a preliminary operation, just that we 'don't appreciate her enough.'

I feel as if I've turned over a rock. The underside of my own psyche is not a pretty thing (they aren't, in general), but I've come rather too close to this particular underside and I'm wondering just what I've been harboring.

A Little Lute Music

I have been to a lute concert. It was billed as Elizabethan, but in fact covered quite a musical range, from Renaissance Italian to Victorian songs and rhymes by A A Milne of *Winnie the Pooh* fame. One soprano, one baritone (somewhat hampered by the acoustics in St John's, but never mind), a violin, several lutes and a gigantic thing called an orbo. It was very good.

We also got a glass of wine and a mince pie in the interval. I looked at the Christmas trees – they are all done now, and there are 51 of them. The church looks beautiful. Some of them were quite avant garde, including the one from the local cop shop which was decorated with police incident tape, like a kind of festive crime scene. CSI Avalon! I spoke to the organist, who is very into interfaith, and we discussed the new vicar: our previous female vicar (a Harry Potter fan) is leaving and there is a hope that the new incumbent will *understand* Glastonbury, that weirdest of interfaith communities (a good quarter of the congregation tonight were pagan and apparently the most supportive mother of a choirboy is, as well). Evidently the bishop is on-side, so fingers crossed.

On the way back, it turns out that the Brue has spilled out onto the road and we have a flood. There will be a hurricane tomorrow, it seems.

Solstice Party

We are having the shop party tonight. I can't remember how many people I've invited and I've no idea how many are likely to show up. At least we don't have a photocopier, which makes it less likely that someone will become rampantly drunk and reproduce their bottom, and the IT person (a disastrous teenager on work placement from the local college) has left, leaving Trevor as the only male staff member and thus minimising the chances of someone inadvertently seducing him.

I suppose someone might put a spell on someone else, which isn't a customary feature of the office party.

A writer friend of mine once remarked that at least when you work on your own, you're not obliged to take yourself up to your office, get drunk with yourself, grossly insult yourself, throw up over yourself and get off with yourself in a cupboard.

Tomorrow, it's the shop dinner, which will at least give us the chance to sit down and eat properly: I've been living off sausage rolls since Friday night. Trevor and I are looking forward to the period between Boxing Day and the New Year, when the rest of the country either pretends to work or just doesn't bother, and we can slob about at home and mutter incoherently and grumpily at one another rather than being bright and sparkly and festive.

Wells

We went to Wells today, which was lovely: very cold and misty with the square towers of the cathedral rising above everything. We have now done the last of the Christmas shopping, both food-wise and present-wise, fuelled by lunch at the County Arms, and cake at one of Wells' rather classy cafes. It's still a novelty to be with a man who actually likes shopping (my late partner's idea of Christmas shopping was to become ensconced in the pub while I did it all, which suited both of us at the time: there is nothing worse – in context – than dragging a man around the shops who just does not want to be there).

Then we came home, canned the radio show and I cooked a guinea fowl, which is an excellent thing to roast, especially if you stuff it with lemons and roast Jerusalem artichokes alongside it. Some regard them as the devil's food. I like them.

We did NOT, however, have stollen for pudding, because the stollen was stolen, by a member of the household who shall remain nameless. Bad dog!

The Cider Farm

My parents are here from Gloucester for the festive period. They are not the only visitors, as we are also hosting Mojo the dog while her owner is in hospital. Mojo's antecedents are murky, but we are guessing at half Rottweiler, half Collie, all nutcase.

She is a rescue dog – we fostered her before, when her current owner (who takes rescues) broke her leg. Mojo is a lovely, lively dog, but also the world's greatest escape artist, bypassing Houdini in her ability to get out of locked rooms, kennels and cages. She is very bouncy – her original name was Jojo, but a friend suggested we change it, as she is always rising.

We went to Wedmore yesterday and did some last minute Christmas stuff, but spent most of the morning ensconced in the George Hotel, which enthused over Mojo and insisted we install her in the public bar – not the usual attitude to dogs round here. Then I drove my parents up the Gothic panorama of Cheddar Gorge and back and in the afternoon our friend P appeared to take the remaining windfalls to the cider farm.

I did not think the farmer who runs this establishment would thank us for taking the apples up on Christmas Eve, but P and I got up there to find a number of people sitting in the barn over mugs of cider in a state not so much inebriated as hallucinatory.

Eventually we managed to establish that Farmer was 'on a trip' and that 'the lad' might be able to help. The lad, who was about forty five, beamed vacantly at me for several minutes before vanishing into the farmhouse and reappearing with Farmer, who may well have been on a trip, but if so, it had been in the comfort of his own front room. 'You'll hate me,' I said. 'We brought apples. Sorry we're so late. You can feed them to the cattle if you want.'

'Ar!' said Farmer (literally). 'I thought I'd be finished afore Christmas but I ent, see?' Then he told us where to put the apples and arranged for a return visit in the next week or so in order that we can be paid in cheese. The local economy hasn't changed that much since Medieval times, I suspect.

Christmas Day

Rosy-cheeked choristers at King's, the flames crackling in the hearth, the traditional merry cry of 'Oh BOLLOCKS!' as I drop half the contents of tomorrow's fruit salad onto the kitchen floor. Ah, Christmas!

Trevor is swearing over a vat of ham and my parents have been eaten by the sofa.

Trevor likes to cook at this time of year and got up early to make sausage rolls for breakfast, bless him. Then I let the dogs out and despite Mojo being in direct sight, she slid through a hole in the fence. Cue fifteen minutes of calling, followed by a leap into the car. I found her halfway down the lane with her trademark 'I didn't mean it! I only! I never!' look. '*Ooo, sorr-eee. I forgot.*' Bundling the dog into the car in disgrace, I returned home to shove the turkey into the oven and went out again to collect a Christmas cake from a friend.

We finally got around to opening presents and I had some lovely ones, including the Druidic Plant Oracle, various books, and chocolates. My mother donated, on my behalf, thirty litres of diesel to the local lifeboat – Trevor is a lifetime governor of the RNLI, which performs a massive service in the Severn Sea, and it's great to support their boats.

We keep losing things. Thus far, a bottle of Glenfiddich and the sprouts have disappeared. I am certain we bought these, but they are nowhere to be found. Last year, Eldest Rottweiler ate half a pound of stilton that my mother had left in a bag. It was still wrapped in plastic. We expected digestive repercussions, but it must have been like dropping the cheese into a furnace: it simply disappeared: 'poof!'

Apart from this, lunch was traditional, punctual and uneventful: it featured one of my cousin's turkeys and a ham, plus the usual vegetables. We had Christmas pudding: it came in a plastic bowl and was microwaved, because like Hell am I steaming something for three hours. Good pudding, though.

In the afternoon, I took Mojo on a long and leashed walk round the footpath at the back of the village – despite a streaming wet night, the late afternoon was cold and clear with a lovely pale sky and purple clouds against a blazing sunset. We saw a heron, lapwings, and the local herd of roe deer, who are sticking around the back paddock despite being chased by our dogs at every opportunity. Fortunately for the sake of my shoulder socket, Mojo was looking the other way and did not see them. There are flocks of wild swans out on the Levels.

And finally we sank into the usual somnolence of Christmas evening. Mojo chewed a wide variety of objects, some lawful, some (potpourri) not. Sid the cat played with his new catnip mouse and went out, after a morning's entertainment in the new bookcase, which has been stashed in the hall temporarily. Sid has discovered that if he lurks on its lowest shelf, he can bash anything that walks past, human or canine. Clearly, this is hilarious.

Supper is in a minute and I'm eschewing the turkey until later and doing marmite on toast, followed by the now-traditional Christmas feature of DR WHO.

AH, CHRISTMAS!

Frost and Birds
Out on the Levels, the frost is lying in the lee of the hedges until well into late afternoon. I had to break the ice on the horse trough this morning and there was a cold, clear sky. The orchard was full of starlings, fieldfares and redwings attacking the last of the windfallen apples, and there were angry wrens in the bramble bushes. In town, all the shops have the usual Christmas tree outside them, mounted on stands set into the wall, and at night the place glows with hundreds of little lights.

Floods
The year is buying time from later on: I went out onto the moors

this morning, and unlike yesterday with its torrential downpours, today was almost a spring day – quite mild and with a high, pale blue sky. The turnpike into Glastonbury has flooded again, however, with the sluice gates at Highbridge closed and the water levels backing up down the rivers and rhynes. Winter's not gone yet. But the birds are stirring: I saw a spotted woodpecker and several moorhens croaking in the bullrushes. We have buzzards in the back paddock and have glimpsed a heron stalking down the ditches. Other visitors include a tree-creeper and redwings, and a herd of half a dozen deer, which graze the orchard in the early morning. Out on the Levels, the marshes are filling with lapwings and the wild swans, Bride's bird, are still here.

January

Twelfth Night and Wassail

We saw in Twelfth Night with the traditional removal of the Christmas decorations in the shops and Imbolc window displays to replace them. I haven't quite finished yet – I'm spending this afternoon in front of the fire, spinning wool for a Bride's Cross, one of the symbols of the Goddess at this time of year, and winding it around cut strips of willow. We're into a quieter time now, not that one would know it – we seem to be as busy as ever, but are spending more time at home working on various things for the shops. I've replaced the pine, holly and mistletoe with hyacinths, white tulips and early daffodils, all of which are coming out in the warmth.

We'll be wassailing next Saturday, with a crowd of people coming over to toast the apple trees in the orchard. This was done many years ago – the orchard itself was planted in 1905 – and we know this because a friend of Trevor's came over with a metal detector on one occasion and located a spoon and a fork, buried upright and used to mark off the quarters of the orchard for the wassailing. We won't, however, be firing a shotgun into the branches to frighten away evil spirits (we haven't got around to having the gun license renewed, apart from any other intrinsic objections). I suspect cider might put in an appearance, and we are owed some – having delivered the windfalls to the cider farm on Christmas Eve, we are waiting to be paid in kind.

Gardening and Birds

Yesterday was beautiful in that cold winter way. We spent most of the day outside, re-organising the woodpile and digging vegetable beds. I have also cleared out the greenhouse, which has given me asthma – something I very rarely suffer from. I wheezed throughout dinner with friends last night. But it's going away, and the wilted tomato plants have all been composted. The rest of the weather is subsequently foul: windy, wild and wet.

Ritual Beasts

A friend of mine recently mentioned the generalities inherent in pagan ritual: the call in some traditions upon the 'hawk of dawn,' for instance. Well, which hawk? There are a lot of different species in both the UK and the States – do we have a specific hawk in mind? Obviously, not every pagan has an interest in the natural world – many practitioners of ceremonial magic do not, for instance, and that's fair enough. But many of us do, and it's good to get out in it – it gives you an appreciation of what's actually happening in the countryside and the landscape around you, and it stops you from being removed from nature and, in consequence, from sentimentalising it.

With this in mind, I took the dog out onto the Westhay Bird Reserve this afternoon – a place TV viewers in the UK will know from the Autumn-watch programme. It's a strange, seemingly lost (but in reality, quite closely managed) area of the county: acres of reed bed and peat bog, haunted by owls and bitterns, mallards and reed warblers, and many other birds. The dog and I walked up through the reserve, past thickets of birch and willow standing deep in water, and investigated one of the hides (for anyone who reads my fiction, this might be familiar from the short story *The Hide*, which appeared in Strange Horizons last year. I'm planning another couple of short stories in this 'Sedgemoor' series).

We saw a great many long tailed tits in the branches – what a friend of mine in Whitby recently described as 'animated lollipops', and flights of small terns wheeling in to take shelter from the heave of the Atlantic storms. As we turned back to go home, the sun went down in a pale burn of gold behind banks of cumulus that looked as though they held snow, and skeins of

Westhay's famous starlings flocked overhead, heading for their roosts in Meare.

I'll leave this account with an image: two wild swans heading east towards the distant Tor, white against the golden reeds, under a high-riding half moon.

The Golden Dawn

I have recently been motivated to do some further research into the seminal late 19th century occult society known as the Golden Dawn. These people interest me, though more as individuals than as occultists, rather as the Bloomsbury set interest me more as people than as artists (apart from Woolf, I have, let's say, grave reservations about the latter). The Golden Dawn arguably possessed more actual talent than the Bloomsbury lot – I think, on the face of the evidence, that Moina Mathers was as good an artist as, for instance, Duncan Grant. Bloomsbury had Woolf, but the GD had Yeats and, by proxy of actress Florence Farr, George Bernard Shaw. The GD was also, as far as one can tell, less obsessed with sex (apart from Shaw and, natch, Aleister Crowley, who thought about nothing *but* sex) – the Bloomsbury set's adolescent preoccupation with semen rapidly grows tedious to the modern sensibility, but Moina's insistence that she would only marry Mathers on condition that they never actually Did It is Victorian in the extreme.

The carnal realm was, according to Moina, 'beastly', which is of course quite true – but only, one is tempted to add, when it's done properly. So was the ironically named Annie Horniman's nervous breakdown when confronted with erotic sculpture in the Louvre, but it was an age that was in the business of finding its boundaries and I suppose these are the extremes of each.

Anyway. My late partner had a working interest in the Golden Dawn. He was a lot older than me and had known people on the esoteric scene in London in the 50s who had known Crowley (forever known sarcastically as Uncle Aleister) and the like. My partner's abiding interest was always in the

Cabbala, but he'd worked as a ceremonial magician for some years and had moved away from it. My own interest in the Golden Dawn, which was inspired by him and by my father (a stage conjurer and product of the Royal Masonic boarding school) grew out of the personalities involved, as I found their actual ritual practices unspeakably turgid. This is a somewhat condescending view – as another friend remarked recently, the amount of time and effort taken to learn what amounts to a six hour play has to be admired. Few people today have the attention span for forty five minutes, let alone anything more serious. I think most of us who have done quasi-GD rituals find them tiresome, but not without power – to quote yet another friend, like doing the run-through of a play rather than the play itself, which is bound to have an element of anticlimax about it.

I'm currently reading Gilbert's study of the rise and fall of the Golden Dawn, which is slightly difficult in terms of chronology, but interesting nonetheless. To anyone who is interested in a feminist perspective on either Victorian spiritualism or 19th century ritual magic, I'd recommend Mary Greer's *Women Of The Golden Dawn*, which is an excellent and sympathetic work.

My ritual heritage stems from McGregor Mathers (i.e. he initiated people, who initiated people, who eventually initiated me). Thus he is a kind of esoteric great-grandfather a couple of times removed – the kind you mumble about at family parties but of whom you are secretly proud, simply because their behaviour was so appalling and because he was, when all is said and done, one of the greatest ritual magicians of the 19th century. Thus, I am interested in the Golden Dawn because, throughout my life, however eccentric, impossible, depraved and silly this group of late Victorian *am drams* might have been, they have contributed to making me what I am, 100 years later. And that's got to be appreciated, at least by me if no one else.

Herefordshire

Kilpeck is on the Welsh borders, sometimes in England and sometimes in Wales depending on the political boundary-drawing of the day. It's a tiny place, with a 900-year-old church that has the most magnificent carvings. Around its roof are corbels – a bunny and a dog cuddled up together, grinning Celtic cats, stags and mermaids and most surprisingly of all, a sheela-na-gig, one of the vulva-revealing images that are found on Irish churches.

The animals were probably taken from a bestiary (the ibex is upside down, after some remark that they fell off mountainsides and onto their horns).

The beast represents those learned men who understand the harmony of the Old and New Testaments, and if anything untoward happens to them, they are supported as if on two horns by all the good they have derived from reading the witness of the Old Testament and the Gospels.' – Bestiary, trans. R. Barber (Woodbridge, 1993).

We went inside the church and saw its ancient font, and the warriors which climb the doorframes. It doesn't feel particularly Christian, with these Celtic and Saxon and Viking influences.

At the back of the quiet churchyard a gate leads onto the mound that once supported Kilpeck castle. Only fragments of the ruined walls remain, covered in ivy and thorn and a huge quantity of gold-green mistletoe. From here, you can look out to the Black Mountains.

There were snowdrops all along the churchyard wall. Imbolc's nearly here.

Talking of Vulvas...

Let's face it, there is a side of paganism which often dwells on the bawdy. It's a path that deals with sex and fertility, after all. The sheela-na-gig is an aspect of this – a popular image in modern pagan circles, and a glorification and reclaiming of pagan imagery and female empowerment. The little sheelas were, historians think, a terrible warning about what you turned into if you showed an interest in sex, and not a powerful female image at all (maybe Moina Mathers was right), but I like them.

However, you can take everything too far and taking it too far is, in my book – unicorn menstrual pads, for 'the vagina that loves magic.'

Don't they all?

The person who drew this to my attention initially thought that the advert meant menstrual pads for unicorns, which would be just *weird*.

And More Unicorns

One of the things that drives me crazy about the New Age, and sometimes paganism, is its tendency to make everything fluffy and nice. I can see why people want to live in a safe and comforting world – I'd even hope that they did. But, unfortunately, nature just isn't like that. Once upon a time, unicorns were savage. They appear in Medieval bestiaries, with other monsters. They're destriers, the warhorses of legend, who kill anyone who isn't a virgin. Fairies steal children, they blind midwives who see more than they should, they seduce you away to a world where time runs away with you.

Angels carry flaming swords and torch your city if you offend the good Lord: they are the eternal warriors of God.

But these days, everything's cute. Everything has the best wishes of humankind at heart. Really?

I know one person who has seen an angel. It had a triangular hat and two faces. It revolved slowly at the foot of his bed, where he lay as a child with a temperature. Years later, he found a representation of it in a cathedral in Canada. It scared the hell out of him.

This tendency to turn the strange and the eerie and the *other* into a Walt Disney creation isn't positive. Or is it just that the new monsters are human? I notice the same tendency among writers of vampire fiction – and it's mainly women who are at fault. It has at its heart the idea that because you are noble and virtuous and probably pure, you can tame that unicorn, that bloodsucker, that dark elf. He (it's usually a 'he') might see everyone else as prey, but you're *different*. He might kill other people, but you'll be safe.

And he'll be watching you all the livelong day, to make quite sure. I can't help feeling that this isn't a particularly healthy approach, somehow.

...And More Apples...

This evening is our own Wassail bash — we have some friends who are going from place to place to wassail, ending up with us. So most of my day has been spent cleaning the house and cooking — loaf of bread, bean stew, apple cake. (The bread came out a very strange shape. Also a curious texture. I have an emergency loaf for the obligatory toasting-tree bit of Wassailing).

The weather was foul, but I took the dog for a long walk this morning to the village post office, and then to a little roadside stall that sells vegetables. I also drove up to the cider farm and got paid, partly in cider, for the windfalls we took up at Christmas.

They're having 325 people for their wassail tonight — a few more than we are!

So, we went wassailing last night at the rural life museum. It was a dark and stormy — oh wait, that's already been done. It was true, though, and we were relieved that most of the festivities were held in the museum's 700 year old tithe barn, which used to belong to the wealthy Glastonbury Abbey. It's a stunning building with a hammer beam roof — very like a church, except for the give-away slit windows.

The band did some traditional songs and then passed around apple cake, in which was concealed a bean. A gentleman got the bean and was duly proclaimed king, crowned with ivy and given a pitchfork with a piece of toast stuck on it. We then processed out to the orchard and a shotgun was fired into the branches of the oldest apple tree (you can, by the way, wassail other things, including bees), nearly causing a Portuguese truck to swerve off Bere Road. The toast was put in the branches, for the robins – the good spirits of the orchards – and cider poured around the roots of the tree. Then we went back into the courtyard for mulled cider and the burning of an ash bundle, bound with willow.

Templar London

Last year, my Druidic order organised a trip to occultist Dion Fortune's old house, now Anton Mosimann's dining club. This was great, and we wanted to make it an annual event, but we are not all fabulously rich, so this year, we did something else instead.

Our tour guide was Professor Roland Rotherham, a delightful man who is a friend of the Order, but not actually in it, as far as I am aware. He is a former member of the Royal Household – he was the person who used to seat visiting dignitaries at royal banquets, and figure out, for example, whether a Persian prince was below or above an English duke in terms of rank. Roland's professorship is in Arthurian and Grail studies (he is originally from Glastonbury) and he is also a former cavalry officer and currently the Stafford Pursuivante Herald (I think I have the actual title wrong: this is the gist of what he now does). He is an elegant, upright man who continually makes me smile every time I meet him ('Do feel free to ask me questions. You'll find me *completely* unapproachable.' Needless to say, this is utterly untrue).

During the tour, we also acquired a Baronet, as one does – Lord Something of Southend. I still don't know quite what he was doing with us; I think he was a friend of someone. Another nice man.

We went around Templar London, starting with the Temple church, an austere building with the classic basilica structure. It was badly bombed in the war, and has now been rebuilt. We had a wander around the church itself, then gathered in the courtyard for a brief explanation of the Templars and their history:

Group member: 'Weren't they arrested for unnatural sexual practices?'

Roland: 'Not at all unnatural to anyone who has been to public school, dear boy! That sort of thing is practically *on the curriculum* up until the age of fifteen.'

Ahem. After this, we went around the corner to the Middle Temple (this is all part of the current centre of law in Britain, for those unfamiliar with the Inns of Court), and into the Middle Temple Hall – this is a stunning building, exactly like the refectory in Harry Potter. It's panelled with innumerable coats of arms, and it has a colossal double hammer-beam ceiling. The screen at the end is reputed to be made of oak from the Golden Hind.

Roland remarked that he met a friend for lunch in this building some years ago and got talking to Lord Denning, who said to him that this was one of the few remaining places where one could have cottage pie and cabinet pudding for half a crown, and free barley water. 'It isn't free,' said the friend. 'It costs 3p.' Lord Denning's face fell and as they left the room and asked the head waiter how much they had to pay, Denning said, 'I've had cottage pie and a pudding. And 2,300 glasses of barley water.' I don't think they backdated it, though.

We had lunch in the Blackfriars pub, a remarkable wedge-shaped building like the Flatiron in New York, but obviously a lot smaller. It is tiled inside, and adorned with metal representations of friars undertaking the seven deadly sins. I couldn't locate lust.

The pub is famous for pies, which were duly consumed and then the additional weight walked off along the Embankment, which was blustery and bright – quite a choppy Thames, too. Our guide Roland then led us around Whitehall, finding soldiers and pointing out items of interest in their uniforms (these are the gentlemen with the bearskin hats, etc). Since he is a regimental member, Roland can get away with things that other people can't, including waving a walking cane at soldiers on duty and divulging details about their underwear, while the soldiers tried unsuccessfully not to smirk. I learned a few things, including the reason for the rather ridiculous horsehair plumes (to prevent a sword cut across the back of the neck, since swords won't cut through horse's tails).

There is apparently some rivalry between the various regiments ('This is a member of the Household Division. Outside, he is calm, yet inside, he hates me intensely.' The soldier did actually grin at this point, but recovered).

We also passed the war rooms, which are reputed to have a nuclear bunker beneath them: Roland informed me that this used to be the headquarters of the British Occult Division, which apparently countermanded Nazi spellcraft during WWII. Who cares if it's true? (although I've met enough people who are in a position to know, who claim that it is). It's a great story.

Then we crossed Whitehall, Roland somehow managing to stop traffic and sweep apologetic tourists out of the way, and into St James. 'Look at him,' said a friend of mine in awe. 'It's like watching some endangered creature in its native habitat. Like a duck billed platypus or something.'

We were shown various places in which Aleister Crowley used to live, and also the site of a flat which used to belong to Roland. It had a cold spot, and later he discovered that this was the place where some aristocratic maniac had garrotted his valet.

This is not, I don't have to point out, the done thing. We were also shown a small former antique shop where members of the Royal Household used to have to visit regularly with a blank cheque, to buy back all the things A Royal Personage had nicked from other people's palaces. Impressively, her *piece de resistance* was the theft of a samovar. Eat your heart out, Arsene Lupin.

Then we went to Buckingham Palace, were ushered through a back door, and taken to see the coronation coach, which is a hell of a thing. It's covered in gold, drawn by a team of about 8 horses, and is, basically, built to impress the peasants.

We're peasants, in the general scheme of things, and it certainly impressed us. Queen Victoria disliked it, apparently, due to its 'disturbing oscillations'. More shades of Moina Mathers…

February

Imbolc

Today has been spent doing Imbolc things – I attended a ritual at the White Spring this morning, followed by a gathering of about sixty people at the Chalice Well. After a tea/hot chocolate break, we all walked down to Beckery, the area of Glastonbury in which Bride's Mound lies: this used, once upon a time, to be the gateway to Glastonbury.

We took the long way round and I estimated that I'd walked about five miles, which isn't massive, but I felt it slightly. I walked in company with a customer of the shop who is becoming a friend, H, an indomitable lady in (I think) her late sixties or seventies who has been an anthropologist and who is about to start a PhD on early domestic tools. H brought a bundle of hazel wands from her garden (you can probably decipher her name from this action!) and after the ritual on the mound, she and I did some guerrilla tree planting along a bramble-infested hedge. They may take, we'll see.

It's typical February weather: not too cold, but misty, grey and damp. Still, the Well was surrounded by snowdrops and crocuses and it smelled wonderful: they have a lot of flowering, scented winter shrubs for the benefit of blind visitors.

I have also been up at the White Spring, where we were shut in darkness for a few minutes until there was a knock on the door and a small child with a snowdrop crown and a lamp entered. At the Chalice Well, there was a brief ceremony around the main pool and then we processed in silence up to the well itself, where they mixed the waters of both springs.

I also went to the weaving class (appropriate, given that Bride is, among other things, a shepherdess). After this, despite the faint threat of snow, I have dug two more vegetable beds, so it's been a productive Imbolc, on the whole. It might still snow, however. We're supposed to be going to Stanton Drew tomorrow for the Druidic ceremony, so we'll see if we're dreaming of a white Imbolc.

Trevor and I went up to Stanton Drew today. It's the second largest English stone circle, after Avebury (Stonehenge is huge, but not wide, if that makes sense). It was a good, brisk ritual, not quite as brisk as my old druid group Anderida's legendary six minute Imbolc ritual some years ago, which took place in heavy rain and was conducted rather like speed-Shakespeare. And even on a raw February day, it's a lovely site; the stones are kept on farmland and we were surrounded by lambs. We drove there and back through Cheddar Gorge, which is spectacular, though the base of it is pretty tacky – it's very odd, seeing a whole tourist industry dedicated to cheese.

Owls
We went to a very interesting talk last night on the subject of owls, by Ann Bryn-Evans. Rather than concentrating on the more contemporary and New Age-y aspects of the owl (people who choose this bird as their totem are sometimes a little too anthropomorphic on the issue), she focused on their actual habits. Ann used to keep owls, and thus is used to having them around the house – rather like cats, they express affection by trying to feed you, and A has not infrequently had to express gratitude for a gift of regurgitated mice ('I lovingly prepared this for YOU – BLEAARGH!'). Perhaps this is not their most endearing characteristic.

We are lucky here in that we quite often see owls on the Levels (usually at a nerve-wracking windscreen height, as they tend to fly low), and have tawny owls out in the orchard. They nest in a hollow apple tree (Trevor occasionally mimics them during their territorial battles and they fall silent: you can hear them thinking, 'That's a bloody big owl. Better shut up.' – and now *I'm* anthropomorphising).

Anne also went into some of the folklore – the idea of the owl as a bird of ill-omen seems to be on the wane, thankfully. Millions of years old, the owl has adapted perfectly to an environment which is changing too quickly for it to keep up – wise it may be (in actual fact, according to A, they are very dim birds), but the species is in trouble in the UK. A great shame.

Countryside

We've had fiery sunrises and sunsets, with frosty mornings and nights. There's a moon lying on its back like a grin in the branches of the apple trees and Orion is striding across the southern sky. This afternoon was warm enough for me to garden in a sweatshirt, but by the time the sun had gone down, it was freezing again. Trevor and I got down to the river yesterday – very boggy fields, since they were under water until a week or so ago. Odd to think that this land was all saltmarsh a few thousand years ago and yet there were people living here in the lake villages, almost in the very spot where we walked.

Pancake Day

We actually had pancakes on Tuesday (buckwheat, with fish roe – the local Sainsbury does not do caviar per se, sour cream, chopped onion and smoked salmon). On the radio show each week, I do a folklore slot, and this appeared on this week's:

'...but by that time that the clock strikes eleven, which (by the help of a knavish sexton) is commonly before nine, then there is a bell rung, called the Pancake-bell, the sound whereof makes thousands of people distracted, and forgetful either of manners or of humanity: then there is a thing called wheaten flour, which the sulphury Necromantic cooks do mingle with water, eggs, spice and other tragical, magical enchantments, and then they put it little

by little into a frying-pan of boiling suet, where it makes a confused dismal hissing (like the Lernean snakes in the reeds of Acheron, Styx or Phlegeton) until at last, by the skill of the cooks it is transformed into the form of a Flap-jack, which in our translation is called a Pancake, which ominous incantation the ignorant peple do devour very greedily.' John Taylor, 1621

There's also a tradition in Scotland wherein you add a pinch of soot to bannocks, thus turning them into 'dreaming bannocks' and giving you the power of divination, temporarily.

Druidic Gorsedd
I went to the annual Gorsedd (meeting) this weekend, which was held near Swindon, at a place called Lower Shaw Farm. This is a sort of city farm in that it used to be a farmstead, but the suburbs grew up around it. They run a lot of courses, as well as keeping livestock, and it's the home of the Swindon literary festival (yes, there is such a thing and it attracts some rather high-level literary people, apparently).

The Gorsedd itself was composed of ritual, meditation, and a trip to Avebury on Saturday afternoon. The proprietors of the farm told us that we seemed 'harmonious', which as I remarked to someone else, was almost bound to betoken a furious row complete with curses and blistering satires. However, we avoided this fate and I made it back to Glastonbury by 4 p.m. yesterday, in time to catch up with a story edit and some other stuff.

Personal incompetency level: high. Not only did I forget to take a coat (in minus 2 degrees) but also got lost and had to ask for help at a kebab stand. This is mitigated by the fact that everyone else got lost as well, but had the sense to leave home earlier than I did.

Ah well.

St Valentine's Day
I did some research on St Valentine's for the radio show last night and all of this is somewhat put into perspective by mention of a gift by some bloke in the 1660s to a court beauty, Lady

Frances Stewart: a £800 ring! In the 17th century! This wasn't, as far as I know, from Lady S's husband, either. The mention is made by Pepys, who would in calculated fashion go round to some higher-up colleague in the naval commission and extravagantly flatter his daughter on St V's Day, as well as hiring a personable young man to go and do the same to Mrs Pepys. The young man would deliver a gift of jewellery, paid for by Pepys (except one year when he was skint, which apparently annoyed Mrs Pepys no end). Eventually they came to an arrangement whereby P's cousin would deliver an annual gift, thus satisfying Mrs Pepys' 'oooh, SHINY!' instincts.

It all seems to have been highly mercenary, venal, and unromantic, so no change there, then.

Queen of the Fairies

I had an appointment in town at lunchtime with a jewellery supplier H (she makes beautiful hammered silver pieces) – we've been dealing with her for some years. I remembered that she runs a 'sacred tattoo' workshop for women – apparently quite a good one, and offered her workshop space at our place. I had, therefore, to tell her that we've got rid of Lodger, whom H knows from the shop. Lodger also did the tattoo workshop.

'Hmmm,' said H. 'I began to wonder whether I'd done the right thing in letting her onto the workshop when we went out for coffee and she told me some stuff.'

The 'stuff' Lodger seems to have told H is this:

– she is the Queen of the Fairies, but incognito on Earth
– her daughter is guarding fairyland in her absence
– her boyfriend is a demon hunter in his 375th incarnation
– when together, they exude such radiance that demons are attracted to them and must be battled off, so they can't be seen in public (when I subsequently mentioned this to people, they all said, 'Oh, so he's *married*.').

H immediately phoned everyone on the workshop and warned them, but as it turned out, Lodger was apparently okay, except that H came into the kitchen to find her slumped over the kitchen table and when she asked, 'Are you all right?' Lodger replied, 'It's the demons.'

She also confirmed that Lodger started bad-mouthing us to her, mainly about the business, which we are apparently running into the ground. Probably we are demons, as well.

I just came home and broke my rule of not-gossiping by telling all this to a friend.

Apparently she knew about the Fairy Queen business. Everyone seems to know, in fact, except us. Had I known we were harbouring supernatural royalty, I might have been more respectful. Or not.

Dogknapped

Over the course of the winter, things changed. Mojo was reunited with her owner and Bear arrived. Bear was a full Rottweiler, with a worried face and a furrowed brow. She wasn't quite the escape artist that Mojo was, and she settled in well – until late in the winter, when she went missing.

I had gone out for the afternoon and our new lodger's girlfriend had let Bear out. She had wandered into the road, and been found. We knew that Bear had been taken away, because a man went into the farm opposite, and asked if she was their dog. They were dealing with stock at that point and so pointed out Bear's home to the guy – but instead of bringing her back, he simply took her. But we were not to find this out until later.

Brittany

Off to Brittany to help a customer assess some shop premises. Our trip was nearly interrupted by a call from an anonymous man, who told me that he knew where Bear was. So I called the police and set a rescue operation into motion.

Slightly delayed, we set off in the late afternoon, into a fiery sunset and a lot of snow. The roads weren't too bad down to Portsmouth, where we parked the car and searched for a restaurant, getting stuck on the wrong side of a non-pedestrian system as we did so. Rather ruffled, we eventually found an Indian place and a pleasant dinner with plenty of time for the boat.

Once on the boat, Brittany Ferries flagship *Pont-Aven*, we discovered that having booked a double berth cabin, we'd been placed in a single. I went to investigate and was told by a very patient Frenchwoman with a cold that the other bed was in the ceiling. Ah.

'You've had to tell a lot of people the same thing today, haven't you?' I said. 'Oui, madame,' she said wearily. Another embarrassing moment in a life that's seen a series of embarrassing moments. Returning, we located the second bed and tottered off to the bar, where we sat watching Portsmouth recede into an arctic distance.

Outside the row of cabins was a bottle of Laphroig in a glass display case, occasioning comment that this might be the emergency bottle of Laphroig: *just break glass*. Also, the emergency bottle of Chanel No 5.

It felt like a smooth crossing, though I woke about 4 a.m. to find the boat plunging like a horse: I gather from Trevor, who in pursuit of a competent crew qualification has crossed the Channel several times in much smaller boats, that there's a rough bit between the Channel Islands (Trevor thinks it's called the Passe de Bretonne but might be wrong). We got up at 6.30, just as the cabin bonged and a disembodied voice told us that St Malo was nigh. By the time we'd actually docked, the sun was up and we had a good view of the city's handsome stone walls.

Our friend A met us and drove us down to Paimpont, which took about an hour and a half. The weather was all over the place, with icy showers followed by sunlight. We spent Saturday driving around Broceliande, which bears much the same relationship to the forest of Paimpont as Avalon does to Glastonbury, with the same Arthurian cast of characters. Paimpont, with its lovely old abbey, is pleasant, and we discovered a Druid ritual in full swing on the shore of the lake – a blessing of the waters and general undine summoning.

We did not interrupt. We went into one of the New Age shops to check out what other people were doing and were attacked by a small mad cat of great charm.

We took a look at a couple of chateaux, including the one in which the Centre for Celtic Studies is located: this sits on the lake of 'Lady of the Lake' fame. Unfortunately, we were then berated by an irate woman with an Alsatian for taking a photo of it, which apparently is not permitted until March. A day out in France is not a day out in France without being lambasted by some officious stranger – I like the French, but there's a particular strain which starts out by being unpleasant and works backwards. I am very bad in this sort of situation, because I smile gently at people and either treat them like lunatics, or behave like one myself, which is easier in a foreign language: it drives people mad. [*A year or so later, T joined the centre's Facebook page and they apologised – apparently the woman we met had been under a lot of personal stress*].

We had lunch at a nice bistro in Paimpont, which had been renovated so recently for its winter season that the painter was actually just packing up. Later, we went to Trehorenteuc, which is the little village where A was thinking of buying the shop.

There's an old chapel, which the local priest, courting heresy, filled with Arthurian paintings.

Broceliande itself is the New Forest kind of forest: quite a lot of open fields, moorland and huge slabs of schist breaking through it. It's a very bare, bleak landscape, interspersed with deep valleys and stands of birch, pine and oak. It is not hard to imagine it as it must have been in Medieval times. Its main industries are, I would guess, agriculture and tourism. The French government seem to have put a fairly big publicity effort into the latter, with good tourist information centres everywhere, but it's still undeveloped enough for an enormous stone circle to have remained undiscovered until thirty years ago, and that only appeared after a forest fire.

On the way back, there is a big convent just off the road. 'Nuns,' A said, quoting. 'They're lovely. What are they *for?*' Also close, is St Cyr, the French equivalent of Westpoint. There was a lot of shooting in the woods, but I think that had more to do with the French love of hunting than St Cyr.

La Motte, where we were actually staying, is a tiny village, no more than one short street, but it is not devoid of interest: it has a communal bread oven, recently renovated, a parish pump, a communal wood store and a lavoir, which people still use (this is a pool, in which you wash your clothes, and some logs to sit on. It was white with washing powder).

On Saturday afternoon the police called me from Glastonbury, saying they had retrieved Bear. Many phone calls later, we arranged for her previous owner to fetch her from the police station and take her to friends.

On Sunday morning we went to Plelan-le-Grand, where there is a weekly street market: stalls selling bread, also cheese, vegetable, oysters, lobsters, sausages and ham, and enormous flat pans of different sorts of paella (by 'enormous' I mean about four foot across). We bought some sausages, some ancient and very expensive cheese which we were instructed not to refrigerate under any circumstances, and some smoked ham. A bought a ready-made local dish which remained unknown until we got home to identify it: it turned out to be a prune flan, a Breton speciality called a 'far'.

After this, we drove back via the Pierres Droites, which is a colossal stone circle in the forest, and back to Trehorenteuc, to see the Golden Tree. Trevor and I don't really get the Golden Tree: it's the stump of a chestnut (I think) that was covered with gold leaf after a bad forest fire some thirty years ago. This seems to have completely captured the French popular imagination. It's impressive and odd, however, and overlooks the Miroir des Fees, a lake at the head of the Val Sans Retour (where Morgan Le Fay is supposed to have imprisoned unfaithful knights, besetting them with hideous illusions so that they could not escape until Lancelot, known for his fidelity, broke the spell. We agreed that being faithful to another man's wife was a slightly stretched version of immaculate moral conduct, but anyway...). We found our way into the valley (Trevor: 'We're heading into a place called the Valley of No Return. What could *possibly* go wrong?'), which was rather beautiful and filled with swift-running iron-red streams, reminiscent of Glastonbury's chalybeate Chalice Well. I did not have the boots for it, however, so we walked for about half an hour and then turned back, with some relief: no hideous illusions beset us although we did meet a rather odd dog.

In the afternoon it rained, so after a short wet walk through the village, we stayed in and cooked.

On Monday morning, it was still raining with increasing force. We went back over to Trehorenteuc for a business meeting, then for coffee with a friend of our host.

After this, we went to Josselin for lunch – an attractive half-timbered town with a magnificent castle set into its walls. It has a large Gothic church with a tomb of some Medieval dignitary (Duke Rohan?). At the feet of the dignitary's wife are two marble dogs, one noble, and one which is rolling its eyes and stuffing its paw in its mouth like something miming vomiting.

During lunch, Brittany Ferries rang and told Trevor that we'd have to sail from Cherbourg, rather than St Malo, due to the increasingly poor weather. Cherbourg is about 3 hours' drive from Broceliande, as opposed to the hour and a half that it takes to get to St Malo. So we were obliged to visit the Tourist Information Centre and log on to find out the train times for Rennes: there was a train for Cherbourg, but it left us with very little time to catch the boat. We decided to go for it anyway, and went back to La Motte.

The wind howled and roared about the little house all night, causing fears for the satellite dish and indeed, the roof, and in the morning, we found that Paris had closed its airports.

The storm had hammered the west coast and there were pictures on the front of the local papers of huge seas off Belle Ile and Finisterre. We caught the train out of Rennes without difficulty, heading up the coast past Mont St Michel and Avranches, and changing trains at a place called Lison. Both the SNCF and the TGV are considerably more reliable than the British rail networks and we were in Cherbourg on time, to find the Pont-Aven sitting serenely in dock. The company put on a car to take us to the boat (bypassing security) and we sailed home.

March

Spring Equinox

Often known as 'Ostara', this is the pagan equivalent of Easter – only without the sacrificial element that is, obviously, central to the Christian mythos. It's unclear where the name comes from: modern pagan convention holds that it is derived from the goddess Ostara, or Eostre, whose name is supposed to be related to 'oestrogen' (it isn't, unfortunately!). But she's only mentioned once, in a text by the Venerable Bede, and might either be a deity of the dawn, or of a German river valley! Later, the brothers Grimm picked up the story and turned it into something more than it originally was. Whatever her origins, the festival that we celebrate is now known as Ostara and associated with the hare and the moon – people often ask me why there are so many representations of the hare in Glastonbury, and it's partly due to the old tradition that witches had the power to turn themselves into hares (the old stories of a man who sees a hare raiding his garden and shoots it in the leg. Next day, granny's got a limp!).

Spring Rain

Last night it rained and rained and rained and rained. The river has flooded up and they've had to open the sluice, which has got rid of most of it. Let's hear it for ancient drainage systems. (We pay £25 a year as our contribution to the county's intricate antiflooding network of channels and rhines). This morning, my Jeep got stuck in the driveway and we had to push it out so that I could get to work.

But the fields are full of wild swans and there is a watery sunlight. The hedges are a foam of blackthorn and bird cherry. The farrier has finally shown up – this is a different farrier to the one who didn't show up (without explanation) last time, although his habit of leaving answerphone messages without actually, you know, leaving his phone number as well (we don't have that system which tells you who rang) has put a hitch in things.

Also had the following conversation:

Me: When can you come?

Farrier: Either Saturday or Sunday.

Me: Which is more convenient?

F: Well, Sunday is my day off.

If some hunting type tells you that they're keeping old rural crafts in business, don't believe them: even finding a farrier who will bother to get out of bed and earn £50 for an hour's work has taken weeks. They're like supermodels. Don't get me started on Somerset Man. Maybe you should just go and see HOT FUZZ instead, which is practically a documentary.

Coming home this evening, through a dark and rainy vale of Avalon, there was a single bright shooting star over the Tor.

Strawberry Hill

Some while ago, our friend and supplier to the shops, artist Anne Sudworth, invited us to a private view of her latest exhibition. This is held in Horace Walpole's old house, Strawberry Hill in West London. We drove up yesterday afternoon, arriving somewhat early, so had a look around the grounds.

The house has a golden griffin and a golden spaniel on gateposts. There's a story in that somewhere. Inside, the place is dilapidated – it's been taken over by a trust, who are in the process of restoration. Anne's paintings are being shown in the dining room and the gallery, a magnificent cloistered room with what I gather is papier mâché fan vaulting. Originally, this was lined in brocade, but they've taken it back to the panelling and discovered a whole set of Victorian graffiti: all the builders' names from 1857.

Anne's work is lovely and this was a perfect setting for it.

Cambridge and Cats

We managed to attend this year's college dinner, at Magdalene in Cambridge, and catch up with our friends Kari and Phil. Kari, as previously mentioned, is a Medieval and Celtic historian and a very good one – she brought out a well-received book on the Welsh princess Nest this year and has a fantasy novel coming out soon in the States. We finally met her cats: beautiful blue-eyed Mooncat, golden Ish, and Horus, who is a nerve-wracked Egyptian Mau.

Ish pees on men he likes. Trevor stopped him just in time.

At Magdalene itself, we immediately received an apology by a complete stranger for wearing a normal suit: his wife had packed the wrong trousers. I refrained with great difficulty from making Wallace and Gromit jokes.

We always seem to find ourselves at these occasions being seated next to eminent clerics. This year, we got not only the eminent cleric whom we'd sat next to in 2006, but also a Professor D, whom I gather is a highly respected Christian historian. He was delightful and on discovering that we knew another historian who has done work on the occult, remarked in piercing Irish tones 'Oooh! Are you a witch?' I don't believe in lying to elderly theologians so replied in the affirmative.

'Splendid!' he pronounced.

Had I told Professor D that I was a practising Satanist, I suspect he would have also replied 'Splendid!' The capacity of dons to take things in their stride is legendary.

Then he leaned closer to me and murmured that he hoped the Master's speech would be brief. 'He NEVER puts any jokes in,' he said. 'I sent him a joke book for Christmas, but he didn't take the hint.' Indeed, the Master's speech was joke-free, but genial and short. After that we started talking about dogs, for some reason: Prof D has 2 collies. ('Much more intelligent than any of my graduate students. And *much* more obedient.')

After dinner we got talking to another don whose name I did not catch, who mentioned David Calcutt's period in office (Calcutt was the Master when I went to Magdalene). It turns out he contacted everyone when they were considering whether to let women in and this particular don, who was clearly not born yesterday in any sense, said 'Typical of a lawyer! You've decided to do it, and now you're just asking us so you can say 'I asked the senior members and we will be admitting women,' – as though they'd actually agreed to it.'

Calcutt admitted it was a fair cop, apparently. No wonder Harold Wilson always claimed he had been glad to leave the back stabbing and Machiavellian deviousness of Oxford for the calm and gentlemanly world of Westminster.

Later on, I met the Master, who told me that when he was about to take up the post, his wife (who is, I think, American) asked if he could take some photos of the college for her mum, who was in her 90s and unable to travel). The Master felt a bit self conscious about skulking about college taking pictures, as he put it, so he went into the porter's lodge and asked if they had any postcards. The eldest porter, a man with mutton-chop whiskers, found some but was rather disparaging – some just showed people punting and not the college at all. 'What do you want postcards for?' he asked the soon-to-be M.

'Well,' said the M. 'I'm about to join the College.'

'Oh,' said the porter. 'What as? You don't look like a gardener.'

'Er, no,' said the M. 'Actually I'm about to become the Master.'

'You don't look much like a Master to me,' the porter said. 'You look much too jolly!'

On the way out, we stopped on the lawn to look at the stars and were joined by another porter, who engaged us in a discussion about witchcraft. I cannot remain in the broom closet: people just seem to know, and as I have said, my superpower is having weird conversations with people. He was very enthusiastic about its nature bias, however.

'Typical Glastonbury'

Last week we met someone who told us a 'typical Glastonbury' story – a German friend of hers booked in at a local guesthouse and paid a deposit, as you do. On arrival, she was told that the owner of the guest house was abroad, but she was well looked after.

On the day before she left, the owner returned and on the following morning, she was given a bill, for the full amount.

'But I paid a deposit,' she said, and produced the receipt, only to be told:

'That was when I was someone else. Now I have a new soul and so you owe me the full amount.'

We had two responses to this – Trevor's was that a punch in the face often offends, whereas I felt that the original contract was with the other person, whoever the hell that was, and therefore she shouldn't owe any money at all. Perhaps I have a new career as a kind of occult lawyer?

As it was the guest argued the toss and left without parting with the second full amount. Interestingly, this connects with an anecdote told to me by a friend who was actually abroad with the person in question: she'd gone out there on a kind of mystical tour, only to be summoned to the group leader's hotel room on day 1 and informed that the real reason for the trip was to magically support George Bush Snr's war effort and to rid the Middle East of its pernicious Arabic presence (!). At which point my friend thought: *oh no* and kept her head down for the rest of the trip, which mainly consisted of Group Leader taking her coterie of young male acolytes into the back streets and throwing a massive tantrum until they bought her jewellery (nice work if you can get it), only to return home and attempt to fleece German tourists of their guest house deposit.

I do, however, plan to try this 'I'm another person now'

tactic with, say, the gas board and see what happens.

Quest Conference

Yesterday, Trevor and I escaped from Glastonbury for the day and drove up to Bristol to attend what turned out to be the 41st Quest conference. This is an esoteric conference which is hosted by author Marion Green, and over the years she's had guests such as Gareth Knight, Colin Wilson, Stewart Farrar, Caitlin Matthews and a great many people who have effectively made British paganism what it is today.

Yesterday's guests were Geraldine Belkin, who runs the Atlantis bookshop in London – an institution that has itself been going for around 86 years and must be one of, if not the, oldest of the capital's independent bookshops – and Ronald Hutton, as well as Marion herself.

We had an extremely interesting day – Geraldine has seen most of the occult scene over the last 30 years come and go, and Ronald gave an equally interesting talk on the difference, and connections, between Witchcraft and Druidry. I would like to issue public thanks to Marion for running Quest for what must be a record amount of time in the history of esoteric conferences (I know some SF conventions have been running for longer, but under the aegis of a committee, not one person). She is remarkable.

We also came home staggering under the weight of rather a lot of books (I refuse to feel guilty) and met up with one of our suppliers – two Welsh-based artists who do Cabbalistic prints, whom we have not previously encountered. And it was lovely to see friends, too.

Pagan Federation Conference

This weekend saw the Pagan Federation conference in Glastonbury – an extremely interesting event. The line up included Damh, talking about pagan music; Emma Restall Orr, discussing pagan ethics; Owen Davies on grimoires and Janet

Farrar and Gavin Bone on progressive witchcraft.

We had to staff the shops in shifts, so were not able to attend all of the sessions, but I did catch Davies and Farrar/Bone. Owen's talk was fascinating – he has a book on grimoires coming out next year and basically discussed 3 magical texts (the *Book of St Cyprian*, the *6th and 7th Books of Moses* and the *Petit Albert*) and their gradual spread throughout the New World. I learned much that I didn't know, including the spread of the Moses texts from the States to West Africa and their eventual influence on voodoo traditions. This was particularly interesting as it highlighted the basically racist assumptions that underly much of Western thinking about voodoo/santeria/candomble etc: e.g. the view of animal sacrifice as quintessentially a 'primitive' African practice. All that stuff about sacrificing black cockerels isn't African at all – it comes from French texts on magical practice. I look forward to reading Owen's book when it comes out and will be hunting down more of his work.

Trevor and I caught up with Emma at lunchtime and did an interview with her. She has a new book out (actually, she has three, but this one is *Living with Honour*, a work on pagan ethics. Emma was largely responsible for training me, so it was good to see her again.

Janet and Gavin, who were staying with us, did a highly entertaining talk on progressive witchcraft. They're trying to take Wicca away from the personality cults of the 60s and 70s – something that Janet obviously knows a lot about, since she knew most of the main folk who started off the various Wiccan movements. Both Janet and Gavin are extremely unpretentious people who are very sincere in what they do: I recommend their work highly, and they take pains to speak out against the manifest stupidities of the Craft (including taking oneself too seriously).

Janet has in fact initiated Trevor as a Grand High Poobah into the Order of Bill the Cat and he will be posting a list of his requirements from worshippers in due course, as soon as he's finished having grapes fed to him by fawning maidens.

April

St George's Day

We celebrated St G's Day with a Medieval dinner at a local restaurant, with our house guest. The dinner was, I find, based on a book by Maggie Black from the British Museum Press (*A Taste of History*) – I'm not sure how Medieval it was (although there were no potatoes!) but it was excellent. We had:

- smoked mackerel
- coddled eggs
- charmcerande (this was a lamb stew)
- smothered rabbit (with grapes and redcurrants)
- a spinach, egg and cinnamon flan
- milk pudding with rosewater
- poached pears

I'm going to try and reproduce the smothered rabbit at some point, ditto the milk pudding.

After this, Glastonbury gears up for May Day/Beltane. We are having a maypole at our house and there is a procession planned for the High St. In honour of the season, we put a five foot high painting of a woman sitting, naked, by a waterfall in the window and a small drum featuring Pan at his, er, Pannest, if you know what I mean and I think you do. This was the Witchcraft Ltd window, which is down a side street and which I am convinced that no one ever sees. Evidently they do, because next day we had a call from the police. Someone had complained and I'll give you two guesses as to which item they complained about – the painting or the drum.

We've taken the drum down.

And you know what? The mother who complained was a pagan. Not entirely sure how she became a mother in the first place, but obviously not by means of a fertility rite.

On Men

Witchcraft is often seen as a women's spirituality, though in the old days, cunning folk were both male and female and it certainly wasn't a province of the latter alone – although the famous witch trials did seem to involve more women than men and this is probably one of the many depressing instances of historical sexism.

The way that Gardner set up modern Wicca was to have a woman as High Priestess and her companion, or colleague, as High Priest, with different functions, and the woman taking the paramount role. Historically, however, this looks a lot like lip service, with the woman conceded to be the goddess' representative in ritual and the man yet still retaining all the power. The result of this is perhaps predictable. We have an example of it here in Glastonbury: when Trevor first took over the witchcraft shop, a lot of women in town objected, on the grounds that since he was a man, he couldn't be a 'proper witch.' This was partly because he fired his business partner, the aforementioned woman once described to me as having 'done one year of Wicca twenty times.'

It may result from different causes, but it's the same old sexism, repackaged and reversed – the same old hungering for power. I'd refer anyone who is interested in considerations of power to Starhawk's THE SPIRAL DANCE: she is still, in my view, the writer who has most carefully and consistently addressed issues and abuses of power within the Craft. I don't, personally, think men and women are all that different. There are people who remain humble and who wear their mantle of authority lightly and with grace, and there are those who crave it for all the wrong reasons. Plenty of both can be found in Wicca, and in Christianity, and in any other religion or group whom you care to name. We're all depressingly familiar with the Wiccan 'guru' who sleeps with his female followers, and with the sufferer of High Priestess-itis, who thinks that because she's done a three year course, it has somehow conferred an innate superiority and entitles her to boss everyone else about (the American web comic *Something Positive* and its psychotic HP, who eventually lacks a coven because she claims to have thrown everyone out of it, when in fact they have left in disgust, is a good illustration).

I would note that it's usually the women who are most threatened by men, and vice versa, who have the most problems with shifting gender roles within the Craft. I have come across rather too many spineless men who can't handle the notion of women in power (*any* type of power), and conversely rather too many women who claim that men can't deal with their 'strength,' when in fact it's their needy, clinging and frequently lunatic behaviour that the men can't deal with.

I'll have more to say about all this later, as it's part of a wider issue. Suffice to say that you can be a witch even if you're a man, and you're not necessarily superior because you happen to have been born into a particular gender, whether that's male or female.

Getteth over thyself, as the ancient magicians possibly did not say.

Damsel Not in Distress

Walking down the High St last night, I was suddenly accosted by St George, in full armour and a sword, who leaped out of the doorway of the George and Pilgrim, exclaiming, 'Ah! A damsel!' I explained that I was not, however, in distress and St George disappeared. But it's the thought that counts.

Lambing

I spent the day on a local farm, who are having a lambing festival. This was arranged by a friend of mine, who wanted someone along to demonstrate spinning. I'm no expert, but I can spin, and so I packed the wheel in the car and took it down to Thistledown Farm, where I showed two little girls and their grandmas how to spin. Okay, the results were a bit lumpy.

The people at the farm are great – they do organic meat

and having seen their animals, we'll be going to them in future as well as some of the other locals. The ewes were in pens and most had either just given birth, or were about to. One of them had literally dropped just as we walked in and had a completely freaked-out expression, as well she might. One of the lambs was a couple of days old, and bouncy. They really are adorable. They had little black faces, rather like our cat, Sid. We also saw three young goats – P picked one up, although it was a bit on the, er, problematic side as far as its rear end went. P, however, remained unscathed ('all in the technique,' she said firmly. P is from Boston and not fazed by much). She also held its mum while the babies fed – Mum is a flighty teenage goat and didn't run fast enough. She stood bleating in panic while the babies homed in like little goat missiles.

Don't Try This at Home

– and today's moment of oddness has been a very artless young man who informed me that taking mandrake gave him a sudden compulsion to ingest his own genitals. I immediately remembered a friend standing in the shop and watching Bear rootle enthusiastically under her tail, in that repulsive way that dogs do, and remarking dryly 'We all would if we could.' I have been hard pressed to keep a straight face.

I told the customer that ingesting mandrake is not a good idea.

Vomiting Jackal-Headed Gods

We have had one very weird episode (even for us) over the last couple of days, when a bust of Anubis spewed about two pints of rancid almond-scented water over a customer (she was apparently remarkably nice about it, as well). Whilst used to stuff of a peculiar nature, this did take me aback, as we can't work out what the substance was nor where it came from (ruling out anything actually supernatural). Oh well.

Coincidence? I Doubt It

Liz was calling on the Egyptian goddess Bast to look after Sid when he went awol earlier in the week. Today I had an email from an old friend, customer and listener to the radio show – who, having not spoken for months, suddenly decided she wanted a Bastet statue from us.

Hmmm...

Yesterday, I was called down from the office to speak to a customer who wanted some healing. Although we advertise it, I have never actually done paid healing in town. No one has ever asked in four years, and we don't promote it heavily, so it was a bit of a shock, and I palmed her and her husband off to the local healing centre. Having never been asked before, I just was not in the right mindset, and as we've never actually done it, the room is not really set up either.

Today, after closing time, a slight but earnest middle aged man walked in and asked for healing, and I nearly said no again. I did not want to do it this evening as I have something else to do – with Bast – in the Magick Box; just something to get rid of a bit of negativity that has been building up in there, which I said I would do on the full moon, so I did not particularly want to have my energy and thought distracted by a healing.

Come back tomorrow, I said – and he will – at mid-day.

Then I asked C how she had done in Witchcraft today – where the tarot/healing room is, and she said – great – and I've got two readings tonight upstairs! So I could not have done it even if I HAD wanted to...

Coincidence? You tell me.

I'm off to see a goddess about a cat.

Visit to the Museum of Witchcraft

We finally managed to get down to the Museum – a few days before they are due to open – to deliver a collection of magical artefacts from the collection of Stewart Farrar.

Although we picked up the collection on our trip to Ireland

last year, we have had to wait till now to deliver it as the museum is only just putting the finishing touches on their new roof – £60,000 and 6 months later!

A wet day to start with, but a good run down and breakfast in the lovely old Castle town of Launceston, before fighting through coastal fog to get down to the harbourside museum. They have an extremely important collection of art and books which are available for serious students of the occult, and a lively and ever-changing set of displays. They are open from Easter to the end of summer, and well worth the time to get down there – a couple of hours from Glastonbury. They need an extra 20,000 visitors to pay for the roof, so make it this year if you can. They also have an online catalogue, and a Friends association.

We offered to transport the stuff for safety – nothing of enormous monetary value, but quite irreplaceable magically, and we had been meaning to visit Janet and her present partner, Gavin Bone, for the last couple of years…

To have our pictures taken for the museum newsletter and the national press as part of the promotion campaign will do us no harm either – but that wasn't the point. As L says, we have in very small way become part of Witchcraft History, and I don't feel too bad about that.

We rounded off the day coming back via Dartmoor, setting out for Wistman's wood – a legendary Elvish wood of dwarf oaks, set high up in a steep valley, and much beloved of poets and artists. It is a good couple of miles from the road, however, and it was getting dark and very cold – so I let L. wimp out, and we turned back to the road after only an hour's hike. We'll go back with more daylight…

May

Beltane

One of the more user-friendly festivals, since it is basically celebrated by having sex with people and this can be worked in around other things... I am joking, slightly.

In our case, the other things are the final-really-this-time end of year accounts, a ton of paperwork, and digging the potato bed, which our magnificent house guests (Mab, Aud and Scott) have taken a hand at. They've also brought me a May garland so as I write this, I am sitting here bedecked precariously with hawthorn and consequently smelling faintly of cat pee (hawthorn not being the most rosily fragrant plant). On the newsboard for this week's Central Somerset Gazette: NEW OWNER OF SEX TEMPLE REVEALED. Glastonbury is so blase that I've somehow managed to miss the fact that we have a sex temple. It is, I'm informed, opposite my hairdresser's.

Lots of Glastonbury actually did get up at 5 a.m. to hike up the Tor, but we were not among them. We'll be having a maypole celebration out here on Saturday and doing our own ritual here. But I did go into town and saw Green Men, female Morris dancers, and assorted pagans up and down the High St. Poems were read, songs sung and hopefully, by now, a maypole erected, with all the seasonal imagery that this invokes.

Very Big Horse

I got home last night to find our maypole celebration in full swing and about forty people occupying the back field. It's a novel sensation to enter your own house to find a large party that you haven't actually had to organise or contribute to. I can live with this.

I arrived too late for the maypole, but in time to jump over bonfires etc (a custom which originally seems to have nothing to do with fertility whatsoever – however, our cattle are now protected). There's nothing like watching several dozen assorted strangers leaping over a fire pit on your property to make you suddenly wonder about the exact status of your public liability insurance. Nothing went amiss, however. Whew.

On chatting to people, this turned out to be an international gathering: several people from Brazil, several Americans, and the Lama Kenpo Rinpoche, who did indeed show up and proved to be a pretty cool dude, relatively young, and wearing shades and a gaucho hat as well as his dark crimson Buddhist robes.

'You have horse!' said the lama.

Yes!

'Very *big* horse!'

Er, yes, he is.

'HUGE! I have two horses in Himalayas,' said the lama, looking thoughtfully at Jasper, Trevor's shire. 'Very small horses! But I could ride that one, no problem,' he added, with the absolute confidence of one who knows that another life awaits if the current one is abruptly curtailed in, say, an English riding accident.

I started wondering about the liability insurance again, also the possibility of being sued by the Tibetan government in exile. I explained to the lama that I had ridden Jasper, but been thrown off, with painful consequences.

'When you fall off in Himalaya,' the lama said, rather dryly, 'You fall VERY LONG WAY!'

He apparently enjoyed himself at this quaint old English May Day rite, anyway, and left me with a string of prayer flags. All of which feature, I now realise, a very large horse. I suspect the Tibetans and Nepalese are like the Kazakhs with regard to horses: the whole of Central Asia is equine-obsessed.

After everyone had left, which they did like lambs at 8 p.m., Trevor and I went to the Ashcott Inn for a late dinner and on coming back saw two little fox cubs scurrying along the verge.

Men in Dresses

The Christians (Pilgrims of Compostela) were fine. They marched and they sang. Overheard outside the shop: 'Oooh, look! Men in dresses!'

Last week, we had the Druids. It's just one lot of men in dresses versus another.

Overheard inside the shop: 'This dress would look so much better if I'd brought my hair.'

MEN IN DRESSES

The Rumour Mill Grinds On...

Apparently, according to a couple of customers today, we're selling all our shops to the man who owns the Gauntlet shopping arcade and moving to Brittany. I've asked a mutual friend to let D know this, as it might be nice if he was aware that he's soon to be acquiring three witchcraft shops.

As rumours go, this isn't a bad one, as it does have some vague basis in the real world (the recent trip to Brittany, and T did offer to buy D a beer the other night). So it MUST be true.

Chelsea Flower Show

Thanks to a friend, who had free tickets, we spent yesterday at the Chelsea Flower Show.

I've been to Hampton Court, as our friend did gardens there some years ago, but never Chelsea itself. Trevor has, because his ex-partner trained as a garden designer, mainly at the Chelsea Physic Garden, and they used to have a stand. The first thing we saw was a huge photovoltaic robot plant, about thirty feet high, whose solar-powered petals open and close with the sun and draw up water from a ground cell. The gardens themselves were beautiful and here are a few of them:

Leeds City Council: this was a Roman garden, harking back to the city's Roman heritage and featuring plants that were brought over during that period. It was a mass of pale blue and lavender and fronds of dill and grasses. It's apparently due to be re-created in an industrial park in Leeds after the show.

The Linnaeus garden: this was an elegant, formal construction with a very Northern feel to it – small pines and grey stone. I was highly amused to read last week's account of Linnaeus' life in the paper – attacked by a colleague on the grounds that his classification system was unChristian and obscene, Linnaeus promptly named a small and insignificant weed after him.

The Fortnum and Mason garden: this had striking blue beehives and an apparently permanent occupation by the BBC, so I did not see it as well as I would have liked.

The New Hall garden: this was designed by the Cambridge women's college and featured Venus in Transit – a pretty garden with astronomical details.

The Fetzer garden: lovely, filled with Californian poppies and featuring the wine company.

There were also some rather beautiful garden rooms, inspired by Hidcote, a Chinese garden with a moon gate and water features, and many more. All were lovely, but the piece de resistance (and best in show) was 600 Days, a Martian garden. It was designed by a woman (Sarah Eberle, IIRC) in conjunction with the European Space Agency, and is supposed to feature the plants involved in a possible terraforming, or under a geodesic dome. There were lots of cacti, carob and calendula, and some beautiful stone paving. We were very impressed by this and so, obviously, were the judges. It's probably going to end up either at ESA itself or one of the scientific institutes here.

Then Trevor and I walked around the pavilion, which was stunning: there were stands featuring masses of carnivorous plants, heaps of beautiful roses, amazing orchids (Trevor's speciality: he used to run a small orchid import business and wants to get back to semi-professional growing, which is just fine by me)... As we walked around, I became subliminally aware of a very familiar noise, a noise unlike any other, but which is so ingrained in the consciousness of anyone who has grown up in Britain that it isn't even anything you pay attention to.

It is the noise of a Tardis, manifesting. Sure enough, there was the familiar blue police box, in a pretty formal garden that turned out to have been designed by... Cardiff Council! Of course. A passer-by (male) was heard to wonder aloud if David Tennant was around, but alas, no... Nice garden, though.

After this, we decided that we'd had enough and we walked up to the King's Road and had drinks in a pleasant bar in Sloane Square, then found a Lebanese place to have dinner, highly successfully. And thence back to Paddington and home.

Initiation

I've been in my Druidic Order for about fifteen years, but when I moved to the West Country, I joined the local division of it, in Bristol. They ask you to progress through the three grades (Bard, Ovate, Druid) again, but much more quickly, so that you get to know everyone. I've spent the last eighteen months doing just this, but was reinitiated last night into the Druidic Grade, where I will now remain. I can't say anything about the initiation itself – not because it is a Great Big Occult Secret – but because this is an experiential tradition and telling people who might join/be members what it involves is rather like giving out movie spoilers.

However, it went very well and I am now re-Druided.

Unicorn

The Druids duly arrived last night for a more general gathering and the ritual went well, except that our Shetland decided he Just Had To Join In and burst out of his paddock to charge into the circle. Cries of 'Ooh, a unicorn!' from the more whimsical members of the group, though anything less like the savage horned destrier of legend than our small, elderly, grubby white pony is difficult to imagine.

Stonehenge

We have two American teenagers visiting us this week, and as they are into old things, I took them to one of the oldest things of all. Stonehenge was much as always, but for some reason, full of beetles. And larks, and poppies, and buttercups. Lovely.

Tintagel

Today a friend and I took our American visitors to Cornwall. By the time we reached Tintagel the sun had come out and it was beautiful: deep, clear green sea, gulls wheeling over the castle and a cloudless sky. The girls and S went down to what might, or might not, be Merlin's Cave (there are several contenders in this eroded coast) and having done this before, I guarded Lourdes the dog ('MUM! Come BACK!'). Then we went up to the castle, an impressive piece of ruin stringing out along the headland. The non-Medieval ruins date back to the Roman period, so before we rule out Gorlois and Igraine, there probably was some kind of Dark Age settlement here. I walked right up onto the headland, from which you get a spectacular view along both sides of the north Cornish coast. The old walls were covered in thrift, scabious, and the little red-and-yellow vetch that I only know as Bacon and Egg.

After this, we separated and S took the girls along the cliffs. I bought a pasty, ate it in the car, then drove to the Witchcraft Museum in Boscastle to interview its curator for the radio show. Graham very kindly gave me an hour of his time and we did a walkthrough of the Museum, looking at hexes and poppets and mummified cats and all the things that contemporary Wiccans would rather not acknowledge. However, to counterbalance this, the curator has had death threats from loony fundamentalist groups, so there's wrong on both sides. As usual.

(It is worth noting that the museum has a lot of local support, due mainly to Graham's own integrity. He is too modest to mention this, but after the catastrophic flash flood which devastated the village in August some years ago, including the musuem, G – who is a coastguard – was out with the locals shoring up the cliffs and rescuing people, rather than saving his own property and livelihood. In maritime areas, this counts for a lot).

They have a rare recording of Aleister Crowley's voice and he sounds exactly like Winston Churchill (my late partner used to know someone who worked in the Atlantis Bookshop years ago and she said that Crowley used to come in and pose, dramatically, with a cloak, until everyone noticed him. '*Well*, dear,' she said to my partner. 'I thought he was a *very silly* man.')

Then it was back to Tintagel and a compulsory cream tea for the girls, after which we drove back to Launceston to get dinner for S and myself. We got home at about 10 and it still wasn't dark.

Madmen

The Tor was apparently cordoned off this afternoon because the police cornered a lunatic with a knife (or an athame, not sure which). We are fairly sure that this is the nut who appeared in one of our competitor's shops yesterday, tried to force open an athame cabinet and was generally menacing. The community police officer had a word with him – or tried to, since he wouldn't communicate except in grunts.

He warranted the appearance of the police helicopter, which costs some outrageous amount of money per hour, so at least they took him seriously. Hopefully, he hasn't hurt anybody, but I will find out more later.

Courtesy of, and copyright, to, the Western Daily Press:

'A Knife-wielding man was arrested by police in Glastonbury yesterday after a five-hour
siege at the top of the town's tor. Police were called to the famous monument at 8.30am after reports from a women walking her dog that an armed man was in the area. They sent in negotiators to talk the middle-aged man into giving himself up. Armed officers and police dogs were also sent to the scene.

A police spokesman said: 'The man gave himself up at 2.15pm and the area was reopened. It had been sealed off in the interest of safety.''

Cups and Swords

Sometimes, as you might have noticed by now, Glastonbury does... stuff. On May Day, I met H, an acquaintance of ours who writes on Arthurian and Templar matters, and he announced that he'd be getting handfasted that day. The actual relationship had been declared the day before, and the decision to get hitched had been made that morning.

Then, yesterday, I was working. Some while ago, we sold a sword on behalf of its former owner, and owed him some money from it. He wanted to come in and collect it, and did so yesterday. In thanks for us selling his sword, he very kindly brought us a present: a little pottery chalice.

I thought this was sweet, and put the chalice on the counter to take home. An hour later, I went out to get some lunch, and ran into the bride in the street. She doesn't know Sword Owner. 'I'm on a mission,' she said. 'We did a ritual on Saturday and we were told that I've got to get H a chalice, and he's got to get me a sword. Don't have the faintest idea what it's about, but that's the deal. Have you got any chalices in stock at the moment?'

At which point I said, 'I think you'd better come down to the shop,' and I gave her the chalice.

Cups and swords. I haven't the faintest idea what it's about, either, but probably we'll find out in the fullness of time.

Beech Woods and Tank Traps

Well – it was different.

H. and D., two lovely people who wandered in to the shop not long ago, had a civil marriage registered recently, and they wanted to commit themselves in a more public and human way, so they asked up to perform their handfasting in a stone circle built by the current incumbent of an organic farm on a beautiful hillside on the very edge of the Quantocks near Bridgwater.

Although we had never actually been to this place, we had travelled up their leafy back lane once or twice. It is very much a working farm so we were not sure what to expect.

The weather was kind, we had a rather rushed but perfectly pleasant lunch in a newly redecorated pub, and Liz changed into her priestess outfit in the loo, to save time. 'Not the first time people have done that for a wedding,' said the landlady!

I am luckier with that. I can generally get away with throwing my robe over whatever I'm wearing.

The farm was delightful, and I had several connections with it. The current First Lady is another Lizzie, who said 'Haven't you got the Witchcraft Shop in town? Didn't you do Sue and Alan's handfasting five years ago in a field on the Levels?'

Small world. Alan, it turns out, still does their timber management for them, and the farm is surrounded by barns with some fascinating timber. The cafe/shop has a range of turned items that I would be proud to have made – all of which spurred me on in my rush to the workshop.

The stone circle has but one natural stone – placed in the East. The other markers are fifteen concrete blocks. Actually quite old ones. Taken (I suspect) from Brean Sands where they would have previously been used as – TANK TRAPS!

Ironic use of recycled materials aside, the space is carved out of the edge of a well managed beech grove, and it is lovely to see sustainable living in practice – the whole farm is run round that ethos, with free running chickens and goats, and various other small scale livestock all over.

But the farmhouse itself has been extensively restored – old 16th century window frames repaired and internal stone arches re-used and incorporated into the modern openplan requirements of a busy function centre. A huge marquee is in place for weddings all summer, and the kitchens were going flat out to provide hot food for the sixty or so guests.

The view north, Hinckley Point power station and the Bristol Channel is spectacular, but they pay for it – 500 feet above sea level and despite strong sunshine it was still fairly cold in the breeze.

To cart us all up the hill was a 40 foot hay trailer – complete with bales of hay for us all to sit on!

A great day for the couple, and as always we made new friends.

The evening was rounded off in the Riflemans, with friend A. providing a rocking blues set for the entertainment. It made me want to get back in to the Back Door Blues Jam sessions up there every Sunday. Oh – wait – that's today…! (Liz: A. also told us that he had indeed been down to the crossroads at midnight, but there was a long queue, headed by Eric Clapton).

Death of a Morris Man
Before we moved to Glastonbury, I used to live next door to

Tom, whose real name was actually Trevor, like mine, and our partners at the time had a hard time separating us. He was in to all things old – tools, steam engines, archaeology, furniture repairing, and I was in to re-using (the word recycling has not actually been invented then), Self sufficiency, and restoring old cars. We were ALWAYS in and out of each others garages and working on 'projects'.

That was in the good old days before the computer took over my life.

Tom raised his head for the first time in many years yesterday. In the mail I received a book list from him – he has always had an active interest in folklore, and I have been meaning to introduce him to Liz for some time.

The book list is almost a thousand items from the collection of a recently deceased Morris Dancer. Nothing of any value, and dozens of 50p paperbacks, but a fatal fascination for a book lover.

From experience I will have to be quick – if I don't get the email in THIS MORNING, I will miss more than half what I want.

Liz looked at it briefly and said – but we don't have any money. It is surprising what turns up when you say that…

An Officer of the Law

Our elderly Alsatian is going to have to be more closely confined. Halfway through the radio show, I looked up to see a disapproving policeman standing at the window. As an offputting occurrence when you are on air, this is hard to beat. I sat gaping out of the window like a carp. Apparently Elderly Dog had been cavorting about in the road. We couldn't see how, because Dog appeared behind Trevor as the policeman was speaking and all the doors were closed, so either the copper let him in or Dog has taken to teleporting. Unfortunately, Trevor chose to disbelieve the policeman, who looked about twelve years old, and they had a heated argument on the patio whilst I, still live on air, tried and failed to give the impression that nothing untoward was happening.

Several listeners emailed in with their opinions on the row, so it was clearly audible.

Needless to say, this did not do a lot for tonight's radio show. Earlier, Bear broke into the neighbour's garden and couldn't get out again: I had to go in and fetch her. I must have taken my eye off her for about a minute. If this goes on, they'll have to be penned.

By a Whisker

One of our regular customers came in yesterday with her husband. She was looking for a wedding anniversary present (for him to buy for her) and likes lockets: we have some nice ones which she had her eye on. She then showed me the locket she was wearing – it was glass on both sides, bound in silver and with a curious horizontal wheel at the top, with which you open the locket. It looked Victorian but it turns out that she bought it from the World Wildlife Fund six years ago! In it was a long coiled white wire.

'I know it looks a bit like a ringworm!' she said, but then went on to tell me that it was a tiger's whisker – her husband works in the tiger house at (presumably) one of the local zoos, and she asked him to scour the ground until he found a whisker, which he did.

When I mentioned this to various people they suggested that had he really wanted to prove his love, he would have plucked the whisker directly from the face of the tiger.

But then again, some people like to live dangerously.

June

Summer Solstice

Some time ago, at a Druidic Winter Assembly, the person who heads my Order read out a description of an aria from the opera Norma, which features a druidic priestess. He expressed a wish that, one day, he might meet someone who could sing it and – being a druid – the gods listened. Six months later, at an order meeting in Holland (my order has about 10,000 members at the last count, all over the world), he met H. And H is an opera singer.

Last night, at the Assembly party, she sang arias from Rigoletto and another opera (alas, I was in the kitchen when she started). Now, what I know about opera can be written on the back of an envelope, but Trevor is well versed in it, having had an aunt who sang at Covent Garden. She was, in fact, the fat lady who sang, at the end of the Proms. I admire the technique, but it is not my kind of music. H was, to my untuned ear, marvellous, although Trevor nearly strangled the barbarian of a sound engineer who thought that dry ice is an appropriate thing to send in the direction of an opera singer.

Unbelievable! The Order apologised to H in public, this morning.

Apart from this, we had a lot of folk, blues, jazz, performance poetry and a rap version of Hamlet. Nothing if not varied.

Be Careful What You Wish For...

Note to our witch friend Laura: if you go to a wedding, and there is an annoying woman who models herself on Victoria Beckham (looking down her nose at anyone who's above size zero and making sarcastic comments about other people's weight), and she is wearing four inch heels, and you think: 'I wonder what she'd look like flat on her backside?' And you then get on the bus to go home and there is Posh-a-like in a cast because she's broken her ankle on the dancefloor and spent the night in casualty... It might not be your doing, okay? It might just be instant karma.

But we're still all highly amused.

We're also highly amused by Posh-a-like's friend, who went up to Laura at another party and asked where someone was.

'How should I know?' said Laura. 'I'm not clairvoyant.'

And the friend looked at her blankly and said, 'No, I know. You're Laura.'

Without a trace of irony.

Activism

As anyone who listens to *The Witching Hour* radio show will know, and as I've mentioned in connection with our Irish trip, we are supporting the Save Tara campaign. This whole thing has been subject to something of a media blackout in recent months, but what you need to know is this:

– the Irish government has, in its infinite unwisdom, approving the routing of the new M3 motorway straight through one of its oldest monuments, the site of Tara and the Gabhra Valley, seat of the ancient Irish kings. Archeological evidence will be permanently destroyed.

– there are alternatives to this route which would prove considerably cheaper and one has to question why this expensive and ill-considered option has been put through (fill in your own blanks).

– no one is against the road per se, but they question its location.

Last night we attended a Tara benefit gig in the Assembly Rooms, which raised over £800 for the campaign. There are people out there now – our friends amongst them – putting themselves in front of diggers and halting the road. The Brits are used to road protests; the Irish are not – they haven't had to be, but now they're learning fast.

Both organisations are running email campaigns and they are particularly appealing to people of Irish-American descent – the more international outcry that comes out of this, the better. An election does not seem to have made any significant difference to governmental opinion. Let's see what shame can do, given that this was, I am sure, intended to be quietly passed through as a fait accompli.

The Bleeping Secret

We don't sell the popular Law of Attraction book *The Secret* in any of the shops and occasionally people ask me about my views on it, and on the other pop-cult phenomenon of the last decade, the film *What the Bleep Do We Know?*

Now, I may be wrong and you are free to disagree with me, but *The Secret* struck me as a case of old wine in a new – and rather pricey – bottle. As far as I could see, the main tenet underlying it was that of standard magic – reality control, if you want to fancy it up, or intentionality. Put your intention into something, via a series of methods like image boards (or spells), and you'll get it. Unlike most magical systems, however, *The Secret* doesn't seem to take that old saw 'be careful what you wish for' into consideration, nor – again, unlike most systems – does it give any hint that you might have to pay for what you get (in ways that are not necessarily pecuniary).

For the record, I do think there's a lot in the idea of intentionality – whether simply because it aids focus, or whether because of more esoteric factors. I've seen it work in my own life to a startling degree – now, again, one can argue for purely psychological factors at work in this (Tanya Luhrmann's early study on how magicians regard coincidence is at the back of my mind here). So I should, perhaps, be a lot more sympathetic to the Secret than I am. However, there are things that ring warning bells – such as the notion that if the system isn't working, you must be doing it incorrectly (instead of the possibility that it might just be a flawed system). I'm not very keen on these methodologies that put the whole onus of failure on the participant. Also, I distrust slick packaging.

The person who first recommended *The Secret* to me (this was, in fact, Lodger, aka Queen of the Fairies) got completely obsessed by it, to the extent that she was watching the whole DVD once a day for a month or more. She wanted, apparently, huge screens set up around the countryside to broadcast it to the population.

Now, admittedly one can't judge a system by its more lunatic adherents (and this did give me a valuable insight into the capacity of some folk to brainwash themselves, not to mention the impetus behind what might be described as New Age Fascism – Orwell would have loved those screens!). But some systems – Druidry, for instance – discourage cultish behaviour, and it seems to me that the Secret has cult-like aspects.

That in itself isn't as sinister as it might sound – I know quite a few people who were involved in early cults like the Rajneesh movement, and some of them are very sane people who cherry-picked what they wanted from the movement, and some are totally bonkers. So I suspect the same is true of this system, too, but I am not moved to investigate it further.

A friend who has been involved in the esoteric for some forty years did immerse himself in it for a couple of weeks, and when asked what he thought, replied that it could be summed up in four little words: *Give Me Your Money.*

Having disapproved of *The Secret*, I was initially much more amenable to the ideas behind *What the Bleep Do We Know?* It's an attempt to marry the powers of perception with quantum mechanics, and this is something I find interesting. My own feelings are that perception – intentionality – does have a lot to do with why magic seems to work (because, empirically, I think it often does, otherwise I wouldn't do it!).

Now, I tread a fine line in my own life. My doctorate, as most people know, is in the History and Philosophy of Science, so I'm used, for instance, to concepts like falsification. I've also undergone a great many experiences in my own life (some of them are in this book) which have suggested to me that there are patterns which go beyond the world we know. Science doesn't have the answer to everything (even if you add a 'yet' to that statement) and responsible scientists don't claim that it does. I'm also interested in connections between magic and science. Superficially, quantum mechanics, with its apparent linkage of perception and the external reality, seems more amenable to this kind of thing than mechanistic physics. However, I also take on board what physicists are wont to say about quantum mechanics: if you think you understand it, you don't. The trouble is that what we think of as quantum theories make great metaphors – even if those metaphors have little or nothing to do with the science in question.

But I'm not sure, on further investigation, that WTBDWK fits the bill. I was underwhelmed to find that physicist David Albert, who is a professor at Columbia, says:

I was edited in such a way as to completely suppress my actual views about the matters the movie discusses. I am, indeed, profoundly unsympathetic to attempts at linking quantum mechanics with consciousness. Moreover, I explained all that, at great length, on camera, to the producers of the film... Had I known that I would have been so radically misrepresented in the movie, I would certainly not have agreed to be filmed.

The examples used in the film are interesting, but when you unpack them, they start to fall apart. The claim that natives, when Columbus' ships arrived, failed to see them, isn't correct. They may have ignored some of the ships they saw, but that's a rather different matter. And the story as a whole may be an exaggeration of a tale told by Cook, not Columbus: there's not even much evidence that this is the case. It's one of those myths, like the phantom hitch-hiker.

The idea that you can imprint words on crystals seems like fun – ugly words produce horrible crystals and beautiful words produce lovely ones – until one learns that the person doing the 'experiment' knew what the words were beforehand and selected the crystal structures accordingly. And the claim that targeted meditation reduced the crime rate in an inner-city area of the US is apparently just not true: the crime rate actually went up and the testimonials to the contrary all come from practitioners of transcendental meditation, who aren't exactly unbiased. The guy who ran the 'experiment' subsequently claimed that it had worked, and everyone believed him, but it didn't.

I'm also somewhat perturbed by the appearance of one J Z Knight, who says she is channelling a gent by the name of Ramtha, a 35,000 year old Lemurian warrior (readers of the cartoon series Doonesbury might recognise the origins of Boopsie's guide, Hunk-Ra). On a fairly superficial investigation on the net, rather a lot of the production team behind this film seem to be associates of Knight. I don't mind a dollop of pseudoscience (the Fortean Times regularly present articles in which some considerable attempt at rigour is made), and I'm all in favour of marrying science and spirituality if it doesn't end in an acrimonious divorce, but I do rather object when easily-falsifiable examples are presented as scientific fact in what amounts to a piece of hype for a cult.

One has to concede, however, that J Z Knight appears to have manifested her own reality to some degree, as she now apparently has gone from a trailer park to a chateau style mansion. I'll leave you to draw your own conclusions as to how, precisely, someone is undertaking the manifesting in this case.

July

Bees and Blackcurrants

A couple of weeks ago, we were given a nucleus of bees from the secretary of the local Beekeeping Society. We taped them securely into their hive and drove them home in the back of the Jeep, one of my more unnerving experiences.

'If they get loose,' Trevor warned, 'Just get out of the car and run.'

However, the bees were calm and we took them to their new home at the end of the orchard in a wheelbarrow.

We went down to look at the new bees last night and they have settled in well. They were all trundling in and out with white clover pollen, which made each bee look as if it was carrying two large laundry bags.

We have also had a ton of fruit – mainly blackcurrants. Trevor has been making jam. I picked about three lbs of redcurrants last night and a few raspberries, but the raspberries haven't done much this year – it's been too wet.

In more exciting news, I was halfway through an email just now when Trevor said, in those don't-argue-with-me tones, 'Open the DOOR! NOW!' So I ran to do just that and encountered him with a blazing frying pan. He threw it into the garden, scattering dogs and cats (far from being alarmed, Sid gave me a 'Whoah, dude! *Cool!*' look, which is typical of Sid, teenage boy in cat's body). Trevor is fine, if slightly singed, but the pan isn't, and it was my favourite omelette pan, too. Still, it's an excuse for a trip to the kitchen store...

Forbidden Knowledge Conference

The Forbidden Knowledge Conference took place yesterday.

Trevor and I were roped in by the radio station and had a hectic day of interviewing all the participants.

We also attended most of the lectures – it was a very interesting day. Tim Wallace-Murphy, who is a wonderfully saturnine gentleman, gave a talk on the Knights Templar. Paul Devereux lectured on spirit roads – he has a book out on this, connecting the old corpse roads with various forms of necromancy and ley lines (not the New Age version – he's gone back to Watkins and they're simply the connecting paths between churches etc). I must look up this book as it's something I find extremely interesting.

Also speaking were Nick Pope, who used to run the Ministry of Defence's UFO project; Ralph Harvey, who is a friend of ours and a senior witch/old soldier; the mother of an alien abductee, and someone from the Raelian movement. The Raelians were all extremely attractive – one wonders if they were selected for this. By the time the Raelians came on, however, Trevor and I had started to fade and so went in search of dinner.

All the interviewing went smoothly and was chiefly notable for how nice everyone was. Epistemologically interesting, too, in terms of examining one's personal beliefs and what one's limits are. I can, for instance, take on board unidentified flying phenomena but not actual abduction. And I did keep wanting to suggest to the mother of the abductee that she simply speak to the Raelians and get them to ask the Mothership if anyone had any records of swiping a child. Or are these different aliens? You'd think such advanced extraterrestrial societies would be able to talk to each other.

The Goddess Conference
The Goddess Conference is in town this week and filled with women celebrating the Crone, as is only right. Overheard in the tea rooms last weekend:

Elderly lady in tweeds 1: 'What IS a goddess, dear?'

Elderly lady in tweeds 2 (at top of voice): 'IT'S A FEMALE

GOD, DEAR!'

Elderly lady in tweeds 1: 'But what do they DO?'

Elderly gentleman in tweeds (in cut-glass tones): 'They prance about in floating dresses and I for one shall not be visiting Glastonbury next weekend!!!'

Goddess Conference: 1. British Patriarchy: nil.

Starhawk

I've attended two of the main workshops and one of the talks at the Goddess Conference, as well as doing interviews with some of the main participants for the radio.

Starhawk's workshop was very good – out of all the pagan/Wiccan non-fiction writers, she's probably had the greatest influence on me over the years because so much of what she writes dovetails with my own perspective (or, to be more accurate, my own perspective has been shaped by what she's written) – feminist, non-hierarchical, environmentalist, activist. She started off her workshop by suggesting that individual action – though good – isn't enough, and global action is too overwhelming. Some kind of compromise is needed, and that's when someone in the audience mentioned the Transition Towns movement which is gathering ground in the UK.

Some of the debate engendered by the Transition movement has become mired locally in issues surrounding the peak oil debate and counter theories concerning climate change (many of which need consideration, in my opinion). This was mentioned, and someone from the local branch of TT stood up and said that they were operating on a 'theory of anyway' – it may be the case that some of the current orthodoxies of the current environmental movement turn out to be flawed, but the strategies suggested through TT were nonetheless worthwhile.

This is an approach I can get behind (although a very earnest lady then leaned forward and said that she'd read on the internet that 'all the planets are heating up!' This may be the case, but engendered a kind of 'uhhhh...' moment in the workshop.

Starhawk very politely said that this may be so, but we were living on Earth and really needed to focus on the immediate environment).

Interestingly, both she and Susun Weed, whom I later interviewed, seem averse to this 'heroic environmentalist' 'we have to rush in and save Mother Gaia' approach (which I rather slammed in my novel *Ghost Sister*). I've always found it a very egocentric – or humancentric – view, on the basis that the planet itself will, if it so chooses, turn itself into a freezing wasteland or a blazing hellhole for millennia regardless of what we choose to do or not do. However, from the point of view of not fouling your own nest, environmentalism would seem to make some sense.

(There was also a question asked about population control, and Starhawk gave an answer which I fully endorse: the principal ethical and practical means of limiting population growth is by empowering women).

Artemisia

The other workshop I did over the course of the Conference was Susun Weed's session on the artemisias. I interviewed her next day and, like Starhawk, she said a great deal that I agreed with.

Local 'alternative' orthodoxy tends towards the vegetarian/vegan, non-dairy, 'pure foods' approach. Now, there is a lot of good stuff in this view. We eat vegetarian meals about three times a week. I love vegetables, especially organic ones, and I love growing them. We buy small quantities of better quality, preferably ethically reared, and therefore more expensive meat (we're lucky to have access to a lot of this – if you're living in the middle of a housing estate in an inner city, for instance, your choices are going to be more limited). I have many vegetarian friends who wouldn't dream of imposing their views on others, for whom I am happy to cook and I am supportive of people with genuine food-related allergies (I have a nut allergy, which isn't psychosomatic and isn't fun, either). But I dislike having guilt trips laid on me by the more militant form of vegan, whether ethical or health-related: I've come across a lot of vegans who are frankly unhealthy and who don't, for instance, go very deeply into the issues surrounding soybean production or the mechanics of food production (the idea that growing crops might require animal fertiliser, for example).

Anyway, Susun also had quite a lot to say on the 'purity' issue: that women, particularly, are encouraged to detox, to see certain foods as somehow purer than others – the kind of 'orthorexia' that I'm now starting to see mentioned more and more in women's magazines. Susun had the view that this is a holdover from a religious perspective that regards women's bodies as dirty and in need of purification – the mortification of the flesh, in other words. It's tied in with the diet industry (detox seems to have replaced diet as a primary concept throughout the 90s and beyond) and with eating disorders generally (the pro-anorexia position is an example: there's no one more holier-than-thou than someone who's starving herself to death). Susun also has the view that both veganism and fasting are actually bad for you – fasting apparently causes the body to let go of organic pollutants that are normally locked up in fat cells, that then just circulate around the bloodstream because they can't be excreted.

'What should we do to get to understand herbs more closely?' someone asked at the end of the workshop.

'Go out and eat a weed,' Susun replied.

'What if it's poisonous?' the person said.

'Well, dear,' said Susun, 'Just eat the ones you already know!'

Dion Fortune

Alas, I fell from grace this morning while passing Courtyard Books (along with Speaking Tree and Labyrinth, one of my favourite second hand bookshops in town).

Steve had a copy of Dion Fortune's The Magical Battle of Britain, which is about Fortune (and other occultist's) war work in combating the Nazis during the Second World War.

It's out of print and it wasn't cheap, but I've never seen a copy before, so I bought it.

The basic premise of their work seems to have been as follows:

— to create a magical network of occult personnel throughout Britain, linked by means of Fortune's weekly letters

— the purpose of which was to open up a channel for disembodied 'Masters' to come through. As a Christian occultist, Fortune's main contact was Jesus, but others included mythological British archetypes such as Arthur

— rather than directly attacking the Nazi leadership, which Fortune felt to be unethical, the aim was to shine an illuminating force on the current climate of Germany, allowing the Masters (e.g. Christ) to do their work. Fortune felt that the 'group soul' of Germany was not innately evil but had become corrupted by ancient and bloody archetypes, and these needed to be fought by more positive archetypal forces.

— halfway through the war, the aim of the group changed, becoming less about the winning of the war (which was felt to be a done deal on the Inner Planes) and more about the reconstruction of Britain, the occupied nations, and Germany itself, which Fortune wanted to see remade as a strong and ethically sound nation.

It's interesting stuff and the tone of it is terribly British, vis this extract:

In our last letter, we asked our members and friends to invoke for the protection of 3 Queensborough Terrace, and in this letter we have the ironical task of informing them that we have been bombed out of it, though without casualties; so it may be maintained that the invocation was at least a partial success, though your Leader and her Librarian look like a couple of sweeps owing to a difference of opinion with the roof, which fell in on them but tactfully refrained from hitting them.

It has often been alleged that DF is a Black Occultist, and we regretfully admit that the allegation can no longer be denied; however it is hoped that soap and water will restore her to the Right Hand Path...

The meditation session was held as usual despite the 'incident.'

'I should like to take the opportunity of assuring our friends that the rumour that I am suffering from a general breakdown brought on by the intensity of my Inner Planes activities in the defence of England does not correctly describe the situation. The trouble is not generalised, but localised in my nose, and the symptoms are those of the common cold. While I would be willing to believe anything of Hitler in the way of frightfulness, I think in this instance he should be given the benefit of the doubt...'

Marvellous!

August

Lammas

We had another two handfastings this weekend – one in Avebury, which would have been lovely had it not poured (and I mean poured) with rain. Sometimes one has second thoughts about this 'nature religion' business! The bride was soaked and so were ourselves and thirty guests, since the ceremony took place among the stone circles. It must have been the fastest handfasting on record and then we took refuge in the Red Lion.

Driving out of Avebury, the car in front of us suddenly stopped and there was a brief hiatus. I knew something had happened when a woman walked quickly past our car with a very odd expression. Then a young girl ran out of the nearby house and gave a quite terrible wail. The guy in the car in front got out and came back with a dog wrapped in a Barbour jacket. It was a German Shepherd, and the car in front of him had hit it. It must have died instantly. There was nothing we could do, but we both felt very bad indeed for the family (and also for the people who had hit the dog – they'd stopped further up the road and were rushing back). Trevor said it looked like an old dog, so maybe sight or hearing had been on the wane.

Yesterday's handfasting – more a renewal of vows, actually – was much calmer and less wet. The couple decided against the Tor on the grounds of the weather and we did their ceremony in the grounds of the Abbey, under a yew above Arthur's grave, and then they took us to lunch.

I was supposed to be attending a Druidic thing last night, too, but the central locking system of the Peugeot locked the petrol cap on and I had just enough to get back home. Infuriating, especially since Trevor knows how to spring the lock, but couldn't explain how to do it (a tiny lever in the depths of the boot). My Jeep is still in the shop having its tyre repaired, so we are not doing well with cars right now.

Back to Tintagel

There is an artist living in Tintagel who supplies our shops, and we went to see her yesterday. We left early and immediately got stuck in the aftermath of an awful crash on the M5 (looked as though a truck had come straight through the barrier and fallen on someone's car: both sides of the motorway were reduced to one lane). However, once past this, we got breakfast in a service place overlooking the huge bleak sweep of Dartmoor and reached Tintagel around 10 a.m. Because I've never been before, Trevor took me to St Nectan's Glen – a lovely narrow path through a wooded gorge, leading up to a spectacular cascade of waterfall through a holed rock, into a kieve, or rock bowl.

It's a stunning, much-haunted place and a friend of ours does paranormal investigations up there. The area is also connected with St Piran, who came over from Ireland on a floating millstone (this was in the days before easyJet), and whose black and white flag (symbolising the shining tin against the darkness of rock, apparently) has become the flag of Kernow.

On the motorway, we passed a crow studying a piece of roadkill. Then I realised the crow had red legs. It was not a crow, but a rare chough, which are supposed to be making a return to Cornwall's coasts. The bird is said to be the bird into which King Arthur changed upon his death.

After buying lots of statuary, we went to Boscinney for a walk on the cliffs and down to the cove – it's a dramatic coastline, with lots of caves and stacks of rock. Then we went on to Boscastle and a helpful meeting at the Museum of Witchcraft, and dinner in the Cobweb, which is an old and moldering pub (in a good way). Good food, too. Got home about 9.30 – a beautiful run back, with a huge moon hanging low over the moors in a rosy sky.

'Does it Work?'

Some twenty years ago, when I was with my late partner, something of vital and critical import to our lives seemed about to happen: it was likely that the local pub would close down.

Disaster!

Being relatively new to the magical world, I decided that the best means of dealing with this impending doom would be to do a ritual to Dionysus (who else?) and ask for his help. I therefore did the ritual – I can't remember the details now, but it involved an offering of wine – sat back, and waited. A week after that, the pub burned down – well, not quite, but the damage was bad enough to close it for a while.

Oh dear, I thought.

When the insurance had been sorted out, however, a new landlord came in – a typical East Ender, a gold braceleted ex-boxer named Danny. He was an excellent landlord and the pub once more prospered. We got to know Danny and his Greek wife quite well, and one night he had a lock in. The conversation got onto the subject of middle names and Danny said, 'You won't believe what *my* middle name is. Had to take it on when I married my wife – her brothers insisted I convert to Greek Orthodox. It's bleeding Dionysus, innit?'

Cue stunned silence. We never told him.

September

Autumn Equinox

We will be heading Snowdonia-wards at the end of the week and I have just frightened myself and everyone else with the reading list for the writing workshop of which I am the secretary. This is the Milford Science Fiction Writers' workshop, now in its 30th year.

I've also tidied the study and my God, this house is almost organised.

Almost. On the domestic front, discovered that the remnants of the soup I made at the weekend had gone off, so I flung it over the wall into the nettles and then looked over the wall to see the cat, narrowly missed by soup, staring at me with an expression of round-eyed horror that said 'What the HELL are you doing?'

Sid has now taken up residence on the other side of the wall, probably in the hope that more soup might be coming his way. He has also taken to dropping in front of the car out of the chestnut tree, as if falling straight from the sky, when we come back at night.

Clovelly

We had to go to Tintagel again yesterday, and we came back via the north Cornish/Devon coast – the so-called Atlantic Highway – which eventually led us down into Clovelly. I've never been here before, and was much amazed to find that it is a privately owned village and you need to pay (£4.95!) to get into it. Having parted with our hard-earned cash, we discovered that Clovelly is (a) incredibly pretty – a tumble of fishermen's cottages with flower-filled gardens along a steep and still-cobbled street, leading down to the 14th century harbour and (b) did I mention steep?

Long views of oak-covered cliffs leading straight up out of the water.

Neither pub was serving food, so we bought hot smoked mackerel buns and ate them on the quay, where we were greeted by a large, hairy, cream and ginger Siamese cat with bulging blue eyes (Cat: *'I require the contents of your sandwich! Kindly place them upon the floor this instant!'*) which we disappointed. Clovelly seems to be full of cats. A stout tabby person with mittens hit me, probably because I took a Liberty of some kind.

On the way back, we tried to find a lovely pub in the back roads near Wellington called the Globe, and lo, we did find it! And lo, it was shut. So we had a decent but not spectacular meal in Wellington itself and then went to a gig in town – Dragonsfly, who are a local band and very good indeed if you like stomping, groove-driven Breton, Albanian, Sufi – or any kind of music, actually. Very varied stuff, though Dragonsfly are such a big band that they took up a quarter of the pub. They'll be playing in London at the Lord Mayor's Festival this weekend.

Hatched, Matched and Dispatched

I did a naming ceremony on Saturday – this went very well. The infant, with impeccable timing, stuck her finger straight up her nose when my blessing was pronounced upon her.

Yesterday, we went to a wedding in Tiverton. Tiverton registry office is an ancient guild hall, with very thick stone walls and ancient oak beams. After this, we wandered around the town for a bit, then went to Minehead and had tea, and then went up to visit the elderly parents of our recently deceased friend M: this was obviously distressing. The funeral is on Monday and Trevor will be speaking at it. M's pitch at the farmer's market was kept vacant this morning, but a lot of people were pretty shocked.

One old lady turned to me and said, I quote verbatim, 'Fucking 'ell. I've only come 'ere for me lentils and 'ere 'e is, gawn.' Pretty much sums it up.

Wart

I have bought a wart. I can't show it to you, as it's currently on the nose of a super-embarrassed 14 year old girl, but I have purchased it in order that it drops off.

This is an old wives' remedy which Trevor tried out on a customer last month: he bought a wart for 10p for a joke and a week later we got a startled email telling him that the wart had gone, where all medical assistance had failed. We ARE a witchcraft business, after all.

How...!

I have a... thing... with machinery. I tend to break it. It malfunctions around me. Successive boyfriends have all, at one time or another, uttered the phrase 'I just don't know WHAT/HOW/WHY you manage to do X, Y, Z.' I've done things to computers that you shouldn't be able to do – weird things, involving the operating system. Ordinary implements just pack up, in odd ways. Where the mechanical is concerned, I am made of fail.

This morning, it was the turn of the laminator. We lost the previous laminator (embarrassing, this, as it's about 18 inches long). Anyway, we bought another one for £9.99 and then, predictably, the lost one turned up. I had to laminate a small poster and since I hadn't used this one before, the following ensued:

Me (to Trevor): You can show me how to use this. Otherwise it will go wrong.

Trevor: Oh, for – look, all you have to do is plug it in, let it heat up, and put the thing through.

Me: I still think you should do it.

Trevor: Just make sure you keep the paper really straight, otherwise it will crease up.

Me: [puts paper through. Trevor watches like proverbial hawk.]

Trevor: That's it. Perfect. Now all you have to do is wait till it comes out the back and make sure it's straight.

Me/Trevor: [*waits*]

Trevor: It's not coming out! I do not know how you manage to –!

Me: But I did what you said!

Trevor: [takes laminator, jumps up and down on it. Laminator dies.]

Me: I'm sorry!

Trevor: And now I am going downstairs to sell £9.99 worth of stuff to replace the laminator!

Me: You know how much your first sale of the day will be...

Sure enough, the first thing he sold was a £9.99 candle holder.

Ask Nicely!

A woman came in yesterday to talk to me about various pagan paths and wanted to know more about Druidry, so I directed her to a few places. She said that she'd seen my own order process up the Tor at the Summer Solstice and had been fascinated: she'd asked someone how you become a Druid and he replied 'Ask nicely!' This seems to have been the thing that sold her on it.

Over on the blog of the person who is the current head of the order, I note a discussion about going on retreat to Iona. Someone asked why Druids chose to go on retreat to a place that has no trees. 'Because we're on holiday,' came the reply.

A Handfasting on the Motorway

We have been in Wales for the weekend to do a handfasting. The bride runs a Medieval bridal shop in Newport. We kicked off the day with a talk for the Library of Avalon conference, which went well, then lunch in Bristol with a supplier, then over the bridge to Wales. Much of Wales could not be seen. Sensibly, the bridal couple changed the location from the forest to the reception hotel and we did it under an awning over the M4 (first time I've done a wedding on a motorway, but the Newport Lodge is high on a hill over the road). The elements competed with the traffic somewhat.

We stayed overnight and had a really nice evening, much of it spent talking to some French friends of the bride's who moved to Newport five years ago (the husband works in a small factory in S Wales which is French owned). They love it and said their neighbours could not have been more welcoming when they moved in, greeting them with flowers and a bottle of wine. I did not like to say that the neighbours may simply have been delighted that they weren't English, as this sounded a little cynical.

It turns out that the bride and groom of the handfasting, who are witches, have been winding up their relations (who are not) by telling them that we were going to do the ceremony naked and sacrifice a chicken. This had the result that twice as many people as expected turned up and I hope they were not disappointed with the rather pleasantly anodyne elemental ceremony that they actually got (in fact, everyone said it was lovely).

IT'S GOING TO BE LOVELY —
EVERYBODY NAKED,
SACRIFICE A FEW CHICKENS,
THAT SORT OF THING

On the following day, we had things to do in Bristol in the evening, so we spent the day up in the Brecon Beacons. We walked round part of Tal-y-bont reservoir (the village has secured a regional development grant and is in the process of building a turbine to generate its own electricity), then drove over to an abandoned Victorian viaduct just north of Merthyr and had a walk there, ending up in Brecon for lunch. In the late afternoon, we called in on my parents for tea, and thence to Bristol.

Interfaith

A young woman has just bounced (and I mean BOUNCED, like Tigger) into the shop and announced that she is part of a Christian youth camp and could she bless me by buying me a tea? Why certainly! They have apparently been sent out to do good in the community, and if this means buying teas for knackered hard working witches, then well and good. I offered her a bag of rose petals in return blessing but she was unsure and declined.

Mog and Bucket

One of our suppliers has just told me that they've christened (or paganed) our newest shop (Cat and Cauldron) the 'Mog and Bucket.' If this isn't a pub, it should be.

Trevor has told her to go and stand in the naughty corner.

Menopause Moments

The scene: myself and a pre-adolescent girl, in one of the shops.

Girl: 'I want something for my sister's birthday. What are these?' (picks up charm, on which is written a witty saying and the logo 'menopause moments').

Girl: 'Hmmm. I don't think she's *quite* at the menopause yet.'

Me: 'How old is she?'

Girl: 'She's 14.' (in a tone that suggests hot flushes are just around the corner for sister).

Me: 'How about a fairy?' (points to range of zodiac fairies)

Girl: 'I'm not sure she'd approve of one that's so scantily clad'.

Priestess of Avalon

6.20: mysterious dark robed figure flits through old farmhouse, mindful that there is a contingent for a handfasting arriving at 6.30.

6.21: dark robed figure catches sight of self in mirror. Thinks: *Fuck*!

6.23: Dark robed figure wrestles ironing board out of closet, rips off robe, irons frantically, prays that no one will arrive and glimpse unmysterious half-naked ironing figure.

I bet this never happened to Morgaine.

Glastonbury Conversations

With thirty-something woman in the street, 7.30 p.m. (she was clutching a can of lager):

Woman: Can I come home with you?

Me: NO!

Woman: Whyyyyyyyyyyy not?

With 7 year old blonde moppet in shop:

BM: Oooh! Voodoo dolls!

Me: No, actually they are Bride dolls. You dress them up in February, in a pretty frock.

BM (pouting): Booooooring! If they were voodoo dolls I'd buy one and set fire to it.

Mother of BM: *rolls eyes*

Me: *resists urge to take child's name and place it on register of future arsonists*

Everything Happens for a Reason

Throughout this diary, you've seen several aspects of our lives, the dark and the light (and the lighthearted). As a druid and a witch, as priestess and priest, Trevor and I hold to the view that everything happens for a reason. I have my reservations about that Threefold Law, and it doesn't work quit as neatly as we'd wish it to – but it does work.

Time and time again, I've seen those who have violated its precepts reap their dubious rewards. And we're not perfect, either. We both have done, and will do again, things which we're not proud of. We'll take the consequences, apologise and learn, because we have to.

Across the course of this diary, I've seen that things do, indeed, happen for a reason.

The lodger who did rituals to make us appreciate her, at the time of Trevor's diagnosis, later came down with a huge goiter in her throat, requiring hospitalization. I didn't curse her, by the way – I didn't have to. Maybe she's learned by now that you really do manifest your thoughts, but if you do, you pay. But for me, the real reason why we underwent all this nonsense was revealed when her family contacted me. Having validation from a complete stranger of their relative's behaviour has contributed toward their own healing, lessening the damaging belief that they might, in some way, have been mistaken.

So the reason might not be apparent at the time, but I've found that it always becomes clear later. I hope that this diary, too, may give someone an answer they've been looking for – or at least, provide them with some more questions!

2007756UK000011B/40/P
UKOW041859171012
Milton Keynes UK
Lightning Source UK Ltd.